POLYMER
CLAY projects

POLYMER
CLAY projects

Create fun & functional objects from clay

Fransie Snyman

STACKPOLE
BOOKS

Published by Stackpole Books
5067 Ritter Road
Mechanicsburg, PA 17055
www.stackpolebooks.com

First published in 2013 by
Metz Press
1 Cameronians Avenue
Welgemoed, 7530 South Africa

PUBLISHER   Wilsia Metz
DESIGNER   Liezl Maree
COVER DESIGNER   Wendy Reynolds
PHOTOGRAPHER   Kenneth Irvine
TRANSLATOR   Amanda Taljaard
COPY EDITOR   Nikki Metz
PROOFREADER   Estelle de Swardt
REPRODUCTION   Color/Fuzion, Green Point
PRINTED AND BOUND BY Tien Wah Press, Singapore
ISBN 978-0-8117-1403-7

Contents

Introduction

I first encountered polymer clay in the late 80s. At the time, I made only large, brightly coloured beads of various shapes and hues. It was the height of fashion to have a string of beads to match every outfit.

The only variations that were considered were changing the shapes of the beads and combining a number of colours to give the beads a marbled appearance that was ever so pretty. A leather string, either matching the colour of the beads or of a contrasting colour, was used to thread the beads. The beads were sometimes varnished, but a matt finish was very popular.

Some bead shops did sell more delicate clay beads with fine detail, but these were usually imported and therefore very expensive.

However, these large, bulky beads were soon out-of-fashion and mine became the favourite toys of my two youngest daughters.

Since then, many new polymer clay techniques have been developed and I recently started experimenting with new fervour. I discovered a whole new world! I realised that the new techniques were really not complicated and thus the purpose of this book is to share them with you. I never thought I would be able to create delicate millifiori beads! The vast variety

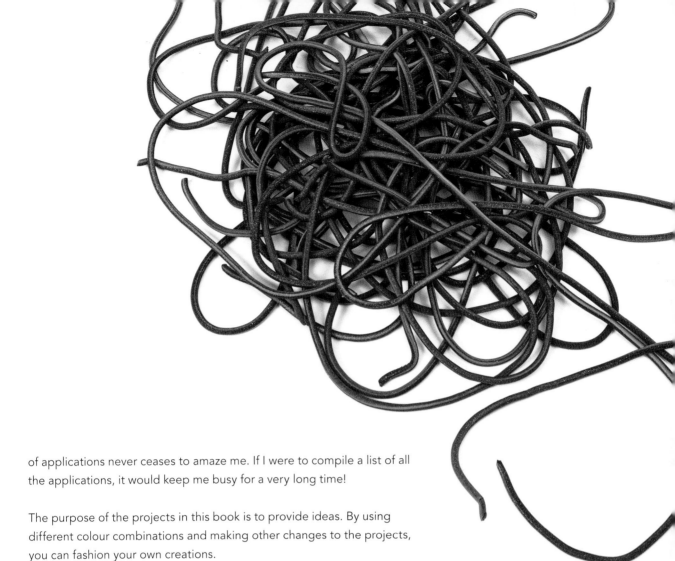

of applications never ceases to amaze me. If I were to compile a list of all the applications, it would keep me busy for a very long time!

The purpose of the projects in this book is to provide ideas. By using different colour combinations and making other changes to the projects, you can fashion your own creations.

Even though there are really not many rules to consider when working with polymer clay, you have to acquire a few basic techniques in order to ensure success. Once you have mastered these, you can make your own rules and add personal touches to your creations to your heart's content. The clay can be transformed into a work of art by the hands of each individual who handles it.

I made many mistakes while working on the different projects; hence, I have tried to point out possible mistakes to you in this book so that you can learn from my mistakes. You may very well also end up with a few less-than-perfect projects, but one learns most from one's own mistakes.

I hope you enjoy the projects in this book!

Fransie

History and types of clay

Polymer clay has been available since the 1930s. It was developed by doll makers who were looking for a strong but mouldable clay for sculpting doll heads. Fimo was the first type of clay to be developed. Other brands soon followed.

Polymer clay consists of basic ingredients such as plasticisers, gel, resin, and colour pigments. The main ingredient of the clay is aluminium silicate, which is soft and mouldable at low temperatures, but hardens when exposed to high temperatures.

The formulae used by individual manufacturers differ slightly and, as a result, the various types of clay have different properties. The best way to familiarise yourself with the properties of a brand is to experiment with the various types and, thereafter, you can decide which clay you would prefer to use.

My personal favourites are Cernit and Premo because they are South African brands that are readily available. The following information may assist you in choosing the type of clay that you would like to use.

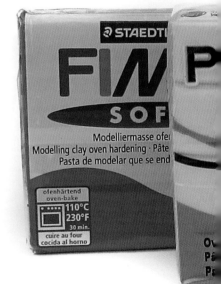

The most well-known brands are Kato, Fimo and Cernit. Filani is a polymer clay that is made in South Africa. All the brands are available in an array of colours, but you can create any colour by mixing the available ones.

Kato clay is the hardest type and the most difficult to condition, but it is the best choice for delicate millefiori work since it does not easily lose its sculpted shape. It is very strong and elastic after curing (hardening), and can be used for any clay work.

Fimo clay is available in two types – Fimo Classic and Fimo Soft. Fimo Classic is also stiff and difficult to condition, but you can achieve very fine detail using this clay. The clay is strong and elastic after it has been baked. Fimo Soft is much easier to condition, but it cannot be used for intricate projects involving very fine detail.

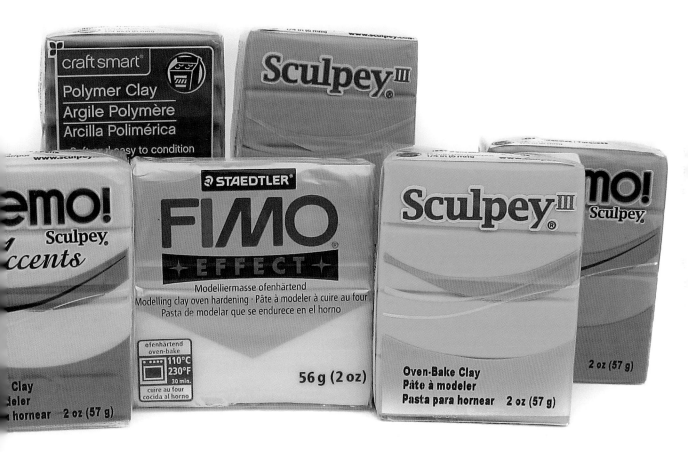

Various brands of Sculpey clay are also available, for example Sculpey III and Premo!Sculpey. Sculpey III is easy to condition and has a soft, matt finish after it has been baked. However, it becomes brittle after curing and it is not suitable for projects that involve intricate detail because it is soft and easily loses its moulded shape. Premo!Sculpey is also easy to condition and is better to use where projects involve fine detail. It is very strong once baked and, although it becomes really hard, it is not brittle after it has cured. Other Sculpey brands are also available, but not as well-known as the abovementioned. I enjoy working with Premo!Sculpey because it is suitable for any project.

Cernit is easily conditioned and is very strong after it has been baked. It has a satiny sheen after baking and is not brittle at all. It is also suitable for any project. One disadvantage of Cernit is that the colour darkens when it is baked. Bear that in mind when you mix the colours for your projects.

Filani is a South African product. Even though it is still being improved on it is already a good clay to use. It is very soft and difficult to use if you wish to retain the very fine detail of your project.

The various brands are available in an array of colours, but you can mix your own colours should you prefer. You can even mix colours by combining various brands. Special colours that contain glitter or a pearlescent sheen are also available in all the brands.

Various brands of liquid polymer clay are also available and these can be coloured by adding pigment powders or alcohol ink. The liquid clay is used to soften hard clay, to affix pieces of a project and to fill the gaps between the pieces. I have used liquid clay for various projects.

For a truly scientific comparison between the various brands, you may consult http://www.garieinternational.com.sg/clay/shop/tension_test.htm. This website explains in detail how various tests were conducted to compare the strength, elasticity, colour changes, and compressibility of various brands.

Crafting tools and materials

You're sure to find a multitude of polymer clay tools, but it's not necessary to buy every tool on offer. You only need a few basic tools, however, I will also discuss the more specialised equipment.

At the outset, the essentials are a suitable work surface, a rolling pin (brayer or roller) and blades.

Suitable work surface

The surface used for polymer clay work must be smooth and should not contain any flaws that may spoil the clay or leave marks on it. A large, smooth, square ceramic or marble tile works well. The advantage of using a tile is that it remains cool in summer, preventing the clay from becoming warm and soft. A tile can also be placed directly into the oven when you wish to bake your clay project.

A sheet of glass, the edges of which have been smoothed to prevent injury, is also suitable. You can even work on a piece of metal with finished edges. A smooth place mat is also suitable, but be sure to place it on a piece of slip-proof material to keep it from moving while you are working.

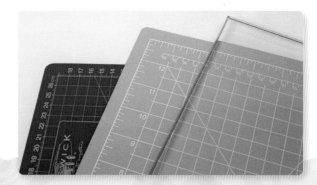

If you have a green or pink, self-healing cutting mat, you can place a piece of tempered glass on it to provide a work surface. It is especially handy since measurements are indicated on the cutting mat, thus you won't need a ruler when you wish to measure specific sizes or lengths of clay. However, do not work directly on the cutting mat, since the clay sticks to it.

A smooth, hard, plastic mat can also serve as work surface, but the sharp blades may damage the plastic or leave marks on it. These marks may inadvertently be transferred to the clay.

When your project involves various parts or colours, index cards are ideal. You can easily shift them around on the work surface and the clay won't cling to them. Index cards can also be placed directly into the oven and, what is more, they prevent shiny marks caused by baking.

I recently came across a glass cutting mat at a craft shop and bought it immediately! It works exceptionally well!

While you are working, wipe the work surface regularly to prevent small, unwanted bits of clay from clinging to a new project. A WetWipe works very well since the smallest bits of clay will stick to the moist cloth.

Polymer clay may affect the finish of wooden furniture. Don't work directly on wooden surfaces since the clay may leave permanent stains on the wood.

Rollers

Besides a suitable work surface, a roller (rolling pin or brayer) is a very important piece of equipment. You don't have to purchase an expensive one. A piece of PVC pipe or glass with straight edges works just as well. It is, however, handy to have a good roller since most projects will require rolling at some stage. Light aluminium rollers and acrylic ones work very well as the clay does not stick to them.

Pasta machine

Should you decide to explore this hobby, a pasta machine is the best possible investment! However, remember that the machine you will be using for your clay projects cannot ever be used to make pasta again – even if you think it has been cleaned thoroughly. Best save it solely for clay. The pasta machine allows you to determine the thickness of the clay when you roll it out since most machines have six different settings. There are machines, made exclusively for clay enthusiasts, which are extra wide and have 11 different settings.

I will be referring to settings on the pasta machine throughout the book. If you don't have a pasta machine, you can use playing cards and a roller to ensure that the clay is consistently thick. Place a stack of playing cards on either side of the clay and then roll the clay until the sheet is the thickness of the cards. A number 1 setting on the pasta machine is equal to a stack of approximately six playing cards (setting 2 equals four cards, setting 3 equals three cards, setting 4 equals two cards and setting 5 equals one card). The smaller the stack of cards, the thinner the sheet of clay will be. You can also use sosatie (kebab) skewers or tongue depressors to achieve various degrees of thickness when using a roller.

Blades

Good blades are very important when doing clay projects. You can make do with an ordinary craft knife that has a sharp blade, or you could purchase blades that are custom-made for clay work. Some blades are flexible, while others are very strong and rigid. Deckle-edged blades can be used to create special effects. When you are tackling tiny projects, small, short blades work well.

Be sure to take good care of the blades if you want them to last! After you have cleaned the blades thoroughly, they can be coated with baby-oil to prevent rust. Store them in wax paper and wipe them before they are used.

Cookie cutters

You are sure to use various cookie cutter designs at some stage, depending on the projects. Once again, you are advised not to use the cookie cutters you normally use for baking. Set aside a collection to be used exclusively for clay work.

Texturing tools

Just about anything can be used to texture the surface of the clay before it is baked. Texture sheets and stamps work well, and a wide variety is available. Texture sheets used for making cards and for scrapbooking can also be used on polymer clay. If you are going to be using a textured sheet for your clay project, clean it thoroughly before reapplying it to paper.

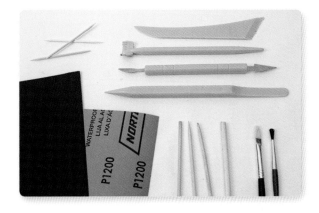

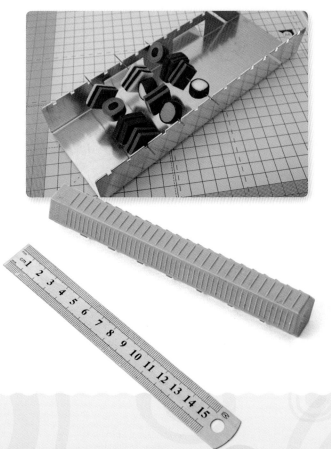

Other handy equipment and materials

Sandpaper, toothpicks, sosatie (kebab) skewers and paintbrushes of various thicknesses are some of the pieces of equipment that I keep at hand when I am working with clay. Sandpaper is used to smooth the edges of finished pieces. Very fine sandpaper is ideal if you wish to acquire a soft, glossy finish. Toothpicks and skewers are used for piercing unbaked clay, and they also conveniently keep the clay beads in position while they are being varnished. Paintbrushes are used to varnish items or to add pigment powder. A soft, small brush is needed to apply pigment powder, while a hard-wearing, larger brush is used to varnish cured beads.

A special, small sculpting knife is a nifty tool when working with polymer clay.

Bead roller equipment may come in handy if you have difficulty shaping the beads accurately or ensuring that their size remains consistent. This equipment is used to shape perfectly round, oval or bicone beads of various sizes.

A special, bead-baking tray is handy when you are making lots of beads. The beads are baked on metal rods that prevent shiny marks on the surface of the beads and also ensure that the beads do not warp during the baking process. If you regularly make beads, a piercing tool (an awl) is the best piece of equipment for making perfect holes.

A polymer clay ruler (Marxit) makes measuring various thicknesses very easy. It is a sturdy, hexagonal, plastic cylinder marked with different increments on each side. The measurements vary from 3 mm to 20 mm. The tool is pressed into the clay and the measurements are clearly indicated on the clay.

An extruder (clay gun) is probably one of the niftiest pieces of equipment that you can use. However, it is a luxury and not a necessity when working with polymer clay. Various types are available, but the one depicted here works best. It is made of aluminium and has a screw thread plunger which pushes the clay into the barrel. An assortment of differently-shaped metal dies (discs) allows you to produce various designs.

The cheaper alternative, which requires you to manually force the clay into the barrel, is difficult to use. If you wish to purchase such a clay gun, I would suggest spending a little more on the better buy.

Special effects can be obtained by using pigment powders and alcohol ink. These can be used to colour clay or to create special effects after the clay has been baked.

Some clay enthusiasts also ensure that they possess an accurate oven thermometer. The thermometers and regulating knobs of all ovens are not necessarily accurate, while the oven thermometer ensures that the temperature of the oven meets the specifications of the specific clay manufacturer.

Equipment for making jewellery

To complete the jewellery projects presented in this book, you will need the basic equipment such as pliers, findings, and stringing material. However, the basic jewellery-making techniques are not covered in this book. For easy explanations regarding these techniques, you may consult the following books: *Jewellery in a Jiffy*, or *More Jewellery in a Jiffy*.

Basic techniques

Certain basic techniques are used for all projects. I will explain these techniques here and, should you not master them at the outset, you could always consult this section again.

Conditioning

All the brands of polymer clay must be conditioned before they can be used for projects. Some brands become soft very quickly while others must be manipulated considerably before they are ready for use. Polymer clay is soft and pliable shortly after manufacturing, but the longer it is stored after packaging, the harder it becomes. When you condition the clay, it becomes easier to work with and the ingredients are once again thoroughly blended to provide strength and elasticity. After the clay has been conditioned, it will remain soft and malleable for approximately 2 to 5 days – depending on the brand.

Conditioning can be done by hand, or by using a pasta machine or food processor.

In order to condition the clay by hand, you'll need to cut the brick or block of clay into thinner slices. Warm the pieces separately between your hands and roll each piece into a thin snake. These snakes can be rolled together once they are soft. Continue rolling the clay into snakes until it is consistently soft and flexible. If the snake snaps when you fold it in half, the clay has not been sufficiently conditioned.

A pasta machine makes conditioning clay very easy. Cut the brick or block into slices, as you would when conditioning the clay by hand. Use the thickest (highest) setting on your pasta machine and run the clay slices through the machine. Combine the slices and roll the clay through the machine a few times. Fold the clay sheet in half and roll it through the machine repeatedly, until it is pliable. If the clay cracks when it is folded, it needs further conditioning. Well-conditioned clay folds easily without cracking.

When you are using a pasta machine to condition folded clay, make sure to roll the clay through the pasta machine folded side first. If the other end is rolled through first, air bubbles will become trapped in the clay. This will weaken the clay, especially after it has been baked and cured.

How to achieve a marbled effect

One of the most exciting properties of polymer clay is the variety of marbled patterns that can be obtained by blending two or more colours in a specific way. You will never achieve the same effect twice!

Follow these steps to obtain a marbled appearance:
1. Roll the clay into thin snakes, using all the colours that you want to combine for marbling.
2. Twist the snakes.
3. Fold the snake in half and twist the two parts.

4. Roll the snake until it is smooth and, should you wish to enhance the marbling, hold the snake at the ends, and twist in opposite directions along its length.
5. Feed the snake through a pasta machine to appreciate the effect of the marbling. The piece of clay at the top illustrates the effect that is created when the snake is given more twists. Be sure not to pass the clay through the pasta machine too many times – you may lose the marbled effect completely.

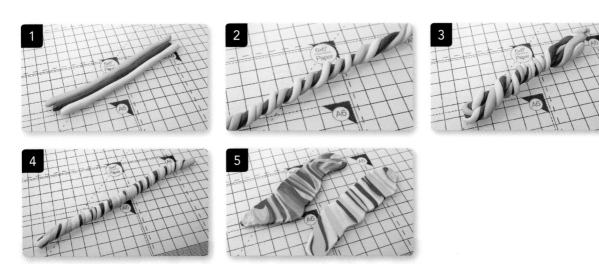

How to mix colours

The different brands of clay are available in a wonderful assortment of colours. However, you can create your own colours to your heart's content by simply using basic colour principles. Special colours that contain glitter or have a pearlescent sheen can be combined with ordinary colours to jazz them up. You can even mix the colours of different brands. Below I have mixed turquoise of one brand with another brand's shimmering white clay to create this beautiful, light turquoise effect.

1. Alcohol ink works very well. Set your pasta machine at the thickest setting and roll the clay that you wish to colour through the machine.
2. Drip a few drops of alcohol ink onto the clay and wait until the ink has dried. It dries very quickly.
3. Fold the clay and roll it through the pasta machine until the colour has been distributed evenly.

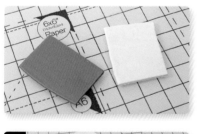

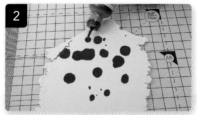
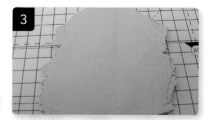

How to make clay roses

Clay roses are made in the same way as icing-sugar roses. To be honest, most icing techniques can also be used for polymer clay work.

The steps for creating clay roses:

1. Roll out the conditioned clay until it is very flat and thin. Use setting 4 on the pasta machine. Decide how big you want the roses to be, and use a cookie cutter to cut circles of clay. I usually use about 10 circles for a large rose (2,5 cm) and five or seven circles for small to medium roses. The circles will form the petals of the rose.
2. Roll up one of the circles to form the centre bud of the rose.
3. Take the next circle and fold it around the centre bud to form the first petal. The edge of the petal can be folded lightly to give it a natural appearance.
4. Fold another circle around the previous two, and repeat this process until the rose reaches the desired size.
5. You will notice that the back of the rose grows longer and longer. Don't worry – merely trim off the excess clay at the base of the rose.

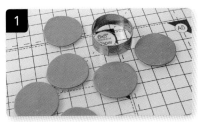

How to create a Skinner blend

A Skinner blend involves two or more colours that are mixed to achieve smooth gradations of colour. It is named after Judith Skinner who developed this technique.

1. Condition the clay you want to use and use setting 1 on the pasta machine to roll out the clay. Cut out matching squares of each colour. The size of the square is determined by the amount of blending that is required. In this example, I cut squares measuring 7 cm x 7 cm, and used half of each square per blend.

2. Cut the squares in half diagonally, but don't start cutting precisely in the opposite corners. Make the incision approximately 1 cm from the top and bottom corners, as indicated.

3. Place the two parts on top of each other – keep the colours separate.

4. Arrange the two colours to form a square.

5. Roll the square sheet through the pasta machine using the thickest setting. Ensure that both colours touch the rollers simultaneously.

6. Once the clay has passed through the machine, fold it in half – keeping the individual colours together.

7. Roll the folded clay through the pasta machine again. Be sure to insert the folded side first.

8. Keep folding the clay in this way and passing it through the pasta machine. You must repeat the process approximately 20 times in order to achieve a true Skinner blend.

9. The gradation after it has been rolled through the pasta machine 10 times.

10. After being rolled through the pasta machine 20 times.

11. Longer rather than wider Skinner gradations are the norm. Trim the sides of the clay neatly and fold the sheet in half lengthwise.

12. Now pass it through the pasta machine, set at its thickest setting, inserting the light side first.

13. Fold the clay in half lengthwise and pass it through the pasta machine again – this time on setting 2.

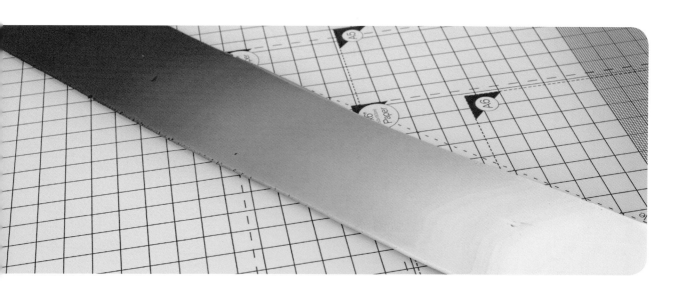

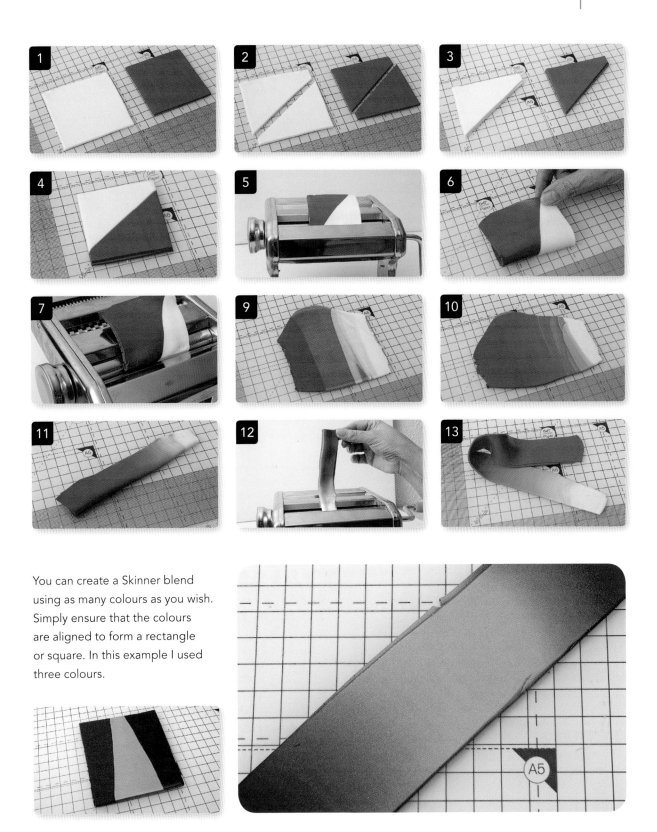

You can create a Skinner blend using as many colours as you wish. Simply ensure that the colours are aligned to form a rectangle or square. In this example I used three colours.

Caning

Making a beautiful clay cane is very satisfactory. You can create a range of canes – from the simplest ones to the most intricate millefiori canes.

In this section, I give step-by-step instructions on how to make a variety of canes. You will soon discover the basic principles, after which you will be able to design and roll your own canes. The most important technique to master is how to reduce the cane. While the majority of canes are round, you can also create square ones.

Reducing the clay cane has two functions: to make the roll of clay that you are using thinner (reducing the diameter) and to remove any trapped air. When you reduce a cane, you have to decide how far you wish to take the process. You can always make the roll thinner; however, once it is thin, there is no way to increase its size. In other words, first reduce the cane to obtain the desired thickness if you know exactly for which purpose it will be used.

When you reduce the cane, always work from the middle of the roll to ensure that the air is forced out towards the ends.

How much clay should be used when rolling sheets to use for canes?

Use one block of each colour for all the canes, since the canes can be stored for quite some time. Reduce smaller pieces of the canes – remember, you can always reduce a cane, but you can never increase the diameter of a reduced cane.

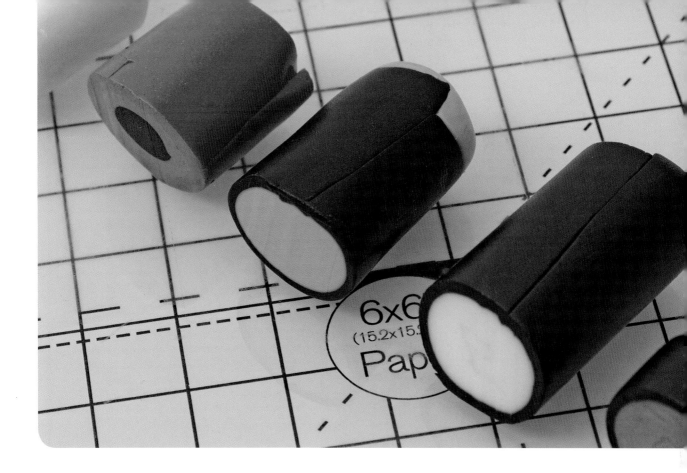

Bull's eye cane with two colours

The bull's eye cane is the simplest one to make. However, by adding a few variations, you can create very intricate patterns.

1. Take one colour and condition the clay well. Roll it into the shape of a log that is approximately 5 cm long and 1 cm in diameter.

2. Using setting 1 on the pasta machine, roll clay of a contrasting colour through the machine. Trim the sides of the clay neatly and then cut the sheet to match the width of the log (first colour).

3. Place the log on the sheet of clay and wrap the sheet around it until it is completely covered. Use a sharp knife to cut the sheet, ensuring that the two ends just meet.

4. Neaten the seam and reduce the diameter to the required thickness. Use an acrylic rod when rolling to ensure that the cane is consistently thick and rolled evenly.

1

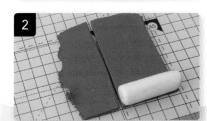

2

3

4

Bull's eye cane with three or more colours

1. Follow the steps on the previous page, but wrap more than one colour around the log. The colours are wrapped around the log one by one, not simultaneously.

2. When you reduce the cane, it usually loses its shape a little. Trim the ends to neaten them.

You can make stunning bull's eye canes using the Skinner's blend technique for the cane and then covering it with other colours as you would any other bull's eye cane. The Skinner gradation can range from light to dark or dark to light.

Another variation of the basic bull's eye is to roll up a Skinner's blend sheet of clay without covering it in another layer. The colour of the roll changes gradually from one hue to another. If you use more than one colour, an even more enchanting effect is achieved.

Bull's eye variation – the lace cane

1. Make a bull's eye cane using three colours and reduce the cane until it is 15 cm long.
2. Cut the cane into five equal segments, each measuring 3 cm.
3. Press these together firmly, shape a log, and reduce it until it is 9 cm long.
4. Cut the cane into three even-sized segments.
5. Reduce the cane to the required thickness.

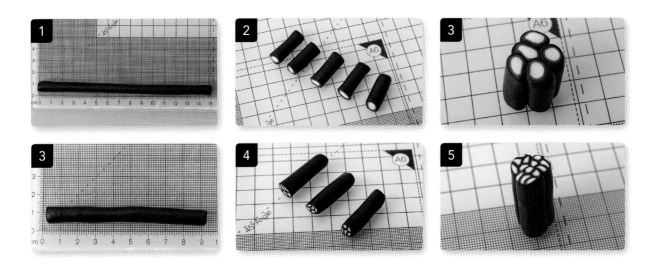

Jelly cane

1. Take two colours and separately run them through the pasta machine on setting 1. Cut each sheet into a rectangle, approximately 5 cm x 7 cm.
2. Place one rectangle on the other.
3. Roll both rectangles through the pasta machine, still using setting 1, until they adhere firmly.
4. Roll up the two sheets to form a spiral.
5. Roll the cane to reduce the thickness and trim the ends neatly.

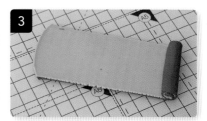

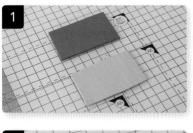

Jelly cane with three colours

You can use more than two colours for a jelly cane roll – it's all the more stunning.

1. Cut even-sized rectangles from three sheets of coloured clay that you have passed through the pasta machine on setting 1.
2. Stack the rectangles and roll them on setting 1.
3. Roll the rectangles into a spiral and reduce the cane to force out any air bubbles. Neatly trim the edges.

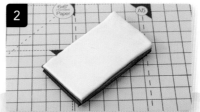

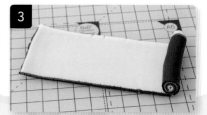

Rainbow jelly cane

This cane looks really exceptional and is not at all difficult to make. You can use either soft pastel colours or lovely bright hues to make the cane.

1. Choose six colours of clay and pass each colour through the pasta machine on setting 1.
2. Cut the sheets of each colour into rectangles measuring approximately 4 cm x 5 cm.
3. Stack the rectangles on top of one another, gently rubbing your fingers over the surface of each layer to force out any air trapped between the layers.
4. Roll black clay through the pasta machine on setting 5. Because this piece of clay is so thin, it is advisable to lay it on a sheet of paper until you are ready to use it. Clay does not readily cling to paper.
5. Cut 3-mm slices from the clay stack containing the six colours, as indicated.
6. Place these slices on the black clay. Be sure to place the first colour against the last colour each time.
7. Use a rolling pin to roll over the coloured slices of clay to make sure that they adhere firmly to one another as well as to the black clay.
8. Trim the excess black clay to match the size of the rainbow colours.
9. Roll the clay into a cane and reduce it to remove all the air bubbles.
10. Neatly trim the edges.

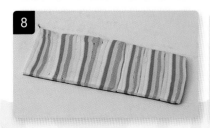

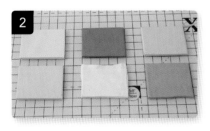

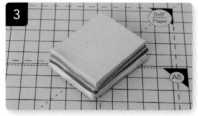

Striped cane

1. Choose two or more colours of clay and pass them through the pasta machine on setting 1. Cut the sheets into even-sized rectangles.
2. Stack the rectangles on top of each other and pass the clay through the pasta machine on setting 1.
3. Divide the rectangles into four or more sections.
4. Place the four sections on top of one another and lightly rub your fingers over the surface to force out any air bubbles.
5. Cut thin slices from the cane as needed.

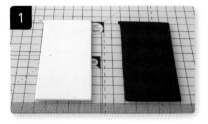

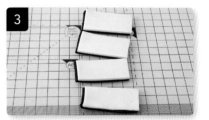

Checkerboard cane

1. Pass even-sized strips of black and white clay through the pasta machine on setting 1. Fold each strip in half and cut it into neat squares.

2. Lightly place the squares on top of each other and rub the surface to force out the air.

3. Use a ruler or measuring bar to indicate 5-mm increments on the clay.

4. Cut the strip into 5-mm slices as indicated.

5. Arrange the strips to ensure alternating black and white squares. In the example, two strips have been placed next to each other and four strips on top of one another.

Quilt cane

The quilt cane is a variation of the checkerboard cane. It simply involves the use of other colours instead of only black and white.

1. Choose four colours of clay and roll half a block of each colour through the pasta machine on setting 1. Cut the coloured sheets into evenly-sized squares.

2. Fold the squares in half and gently press them together. Do not apply too much pressure.

3. Cut 5-mm strips from the clay stack.

4. Use four of the strips and peel off the colours as indicated. Peel off the top colour of the first strip; the top two colours of the second strip; and only the bottom colour of the third strip.

5. The strips are now stacked on top of one another again so that the positions of the colours change as each consecutive layer is added. Follow the steps indicated in the photos:

6. Press the strip that contains three layers onto the strip that still contains all the colours. The colours must form a step pattern.

7. Press the strip containing two colours onto the strip containing three colours.

8. The single, dark colour is placed on top of the strip with two colours.

9. Start filling the 'steps' from the bottom by adding a single light strip.

10. Next, add the strip containing two light colours.

11. Lastly, place the remaining strip of clay on top of the other strips to complete the step pattern.

12. Press the strips firmly together and reduce the cane to a length of approximately 5 cm. Trim the edges neatly.

13. Cut the cane in half lengthwise .

14. Place the two halves against each other, ensuring that the same colours meet.

15. Cut this section in half again (from the top) lengthwise .

16. Lay two halves flat and press them together to obtain the quilt pattern. You can create two combinations.

17. Reduce this square to a long cane and neatly trim the edges.

18. To reduce a square into a cane, use a rolling pin to even each side in turn while maintaining the shape. Turn the cane once one side has been reduced.

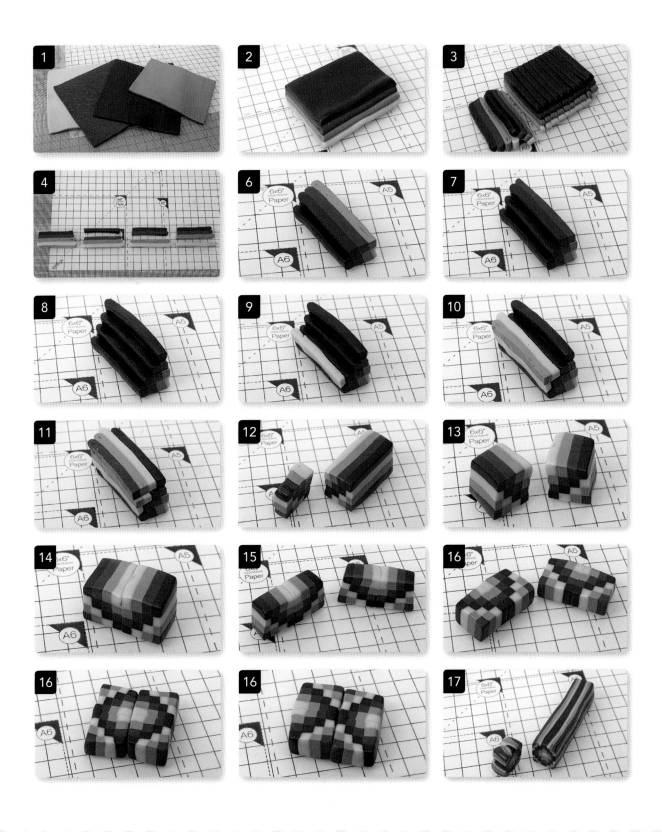

Mosaic cane

1. Use a quarter block each of five different colours and shape logs of approximately 5 cm long and 1 cm in diameter. These measurements serve merely as a guide; the dimensions don't have to be this precise. Just ensure that all the logs are the same size.
2. Condition the clay and pass half a square of white clay through the pasta machine on setting 2. Make four bull's eye canes using the five colours.
3. Reduce all the canes slightly and trim the edges neatly.
4. Press them together and shape one new log.
5. Reduce this cane and trim the edges.
6. Place the cane in an upright position and cut it in half lengthwise.
7. Cover one of the cut edges with white clay that has been passed through the pasta machine on setting 1.
8. Press the two sides against each other again, but flip one of them vertically.
9. Cut the cane in half lengthwise at another spot. Try to cut through at least two colours.
10. Once again, cover one side with white clay that has been passed through the pasta machine on setting 1.
11. Repeat the process at least once, or more than once should you prefer.
12. Reduce the cane. You can reduce it to a square or leave it round.
13. Use a clay roller if you want to reduce it to form a square cane.

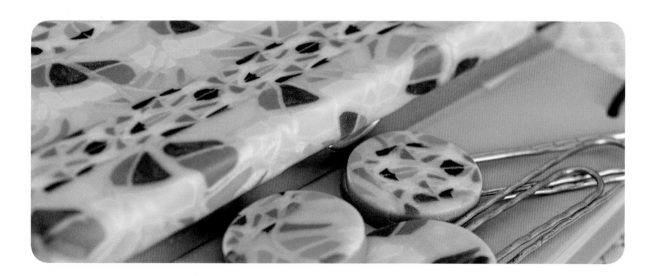

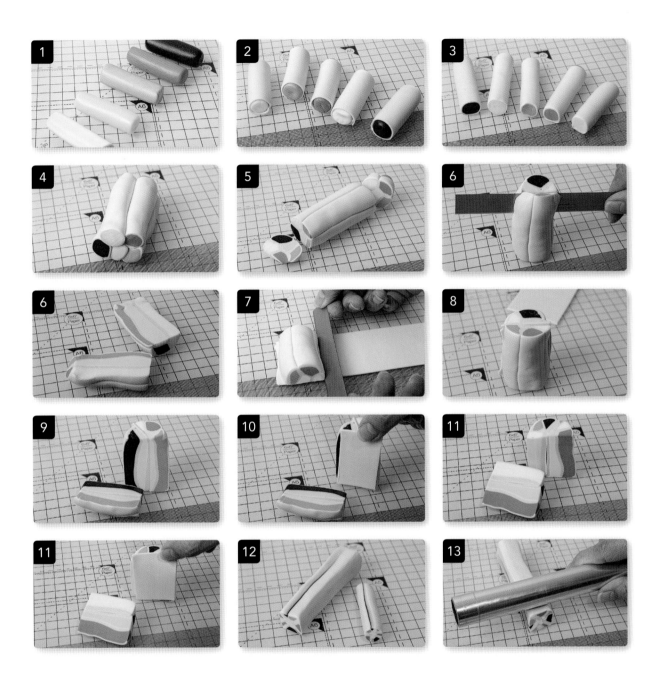

Retro cane

1. Decide which colours you would like to use and roll three logs that are approximately 4,5 cm long with a diameter of 1,5 cm. The logs must have the same diameter as your extruder or clay gun. You may opt to use more than three colours.

2. Cut each of the logs into slices that are 5 mm thick. You should have about eight or nine slices.

3. Arrange the slices alternating the colours and press them together into a firm log.

4. Place the log into the barrel of the extruder and use the square die when you extrude the clay.

5. Divide the extruded strip into 16 equal segments. It works well if you first cut the strip in half and then divide each half into quarters.

6. Arrange the 16 segments into groups of four.

7. Stack the groups of four on top of one another to form a cube.

8. Roll and reduce the cube to obtain the desired size and neatly trim the edges.

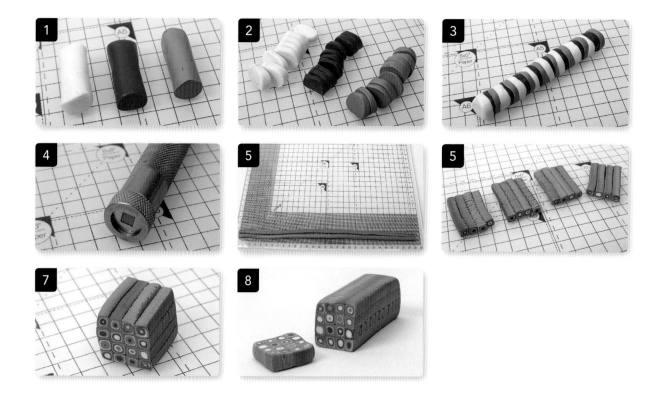

Brain cane

1. Create a Skinner blend using three colours. I used half a block each of red, blue and gold clay.

2. Prepare two strips of black and one white strip as follows: roll the white and one of the black strips through the pasta machine on setting 1, and use setting 4 for the second black strip.

3. Place the thicker black strip, the white and then the thinner black strip on top of one another and run the stack through the pasta machine on setting 1.

4. Place the Skinner blend on the black-and-white strip of clay and run it through the pasta machine on setting 1.

5. Trim the edges of the strip neatly and then begin to roll up the strip. Make zigzag or fan folds while you are rolling up the clay, as indicated. Make sure that the outside edge of the cane is always black.

6. Continue folding and rolling until the entire strip has been used. Reduce the cane to the desired diameter and neatly trim the edges.

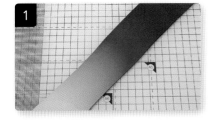

Square cane with simple pattern

1. Use half a block of black clay and roll it into a log. Reduce the log to approximately 3 cm x 2 cm x 2 cm. Set the extra black clay aside for later use.

2. Cut approximately 1 cm from the front end of the log.

3. Run a piece of blue clay through the pasta machine on setting 1 and press this onto the cut edge. Replace the 1 cm that was cut off.

4. Make three cuts lengthwise.

5. Run the pieces of pink and purple clay through the pasta machine on setting 1 and press these colours onto the cut edges. Press all the segments into position.

6. Cut approximately 1 cm from the rear end of the bar.

7. Press a piece of turquoise clay, that was run through the pasta machine on setting 1, onto the cut edge and compress the clay.

8. Reduce the cane to get rid of any air, and then neatly trim the edges.

9. Run a quarter of a block of bright pink clay through the pasta machine on setting 1.

10. Trim the pink clay to match the black and wrap the black bar in the pink sheet, as you would when making a bull's eye cane.

11. Run the black clay, left over after shaping the bar, through the pasta machine on setting 2. Cut this to the width of the cane and cover the cane with it.

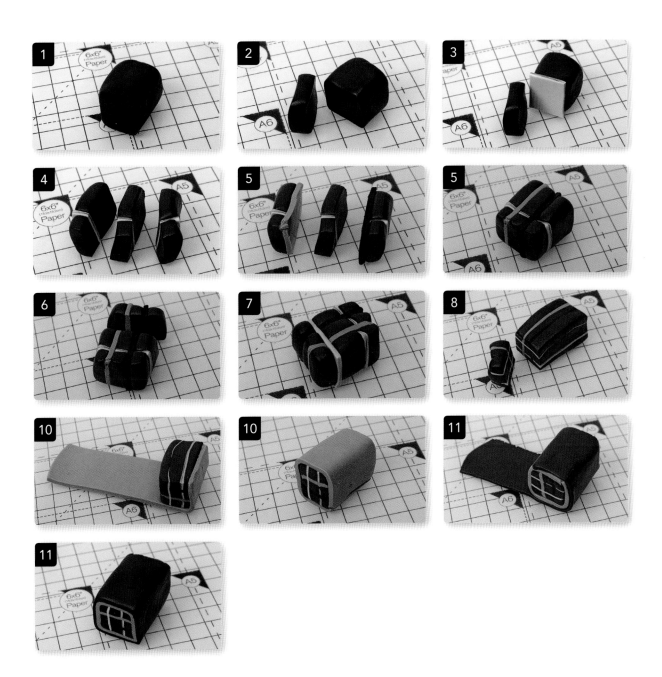

Millefiori canes

Millefiori canes are little works of art that take shape step by detailed step. The technique is derived from glass work – glass makers fashion beautiful, delicate flowers using coloured pieces of glass. The technique has recently been applied to polymer clay. The clay is malleable without having to be heated and it is, therefore, easier to create intricate millefiori patterns using clay as a medium rather than glass.

Abstract flower cane

1. Use one block each of white and bright pink clay to create a blended cane (using the Skinner technique).
2. Roll up the sheet starting at the white end.
3. Reduce the cane to a length of 18 cm (it must be 18 cm long after the ends have been trimmed).
4. Divide the cane into three pieces measuring 6 cm each.
5. Reduce one of the pieces to 12 cm in length.
6. You now have two canes of 6 cm each and one of 12 cm.
7. Divide the 12-cm cane into four equal pieces measuring 3 cm each.
8. Cut three of the 3-cm canes in half lengthwise.
9. Arrange the canes that have been halved around the one that hasn't been cut.
10. Cut the 6-cm canes in half so that you have four canes measuring 3 cm each.
11. Make three evenly spaced cuts lengthwise to divide these canes into three equal pieces.
12. Flatten the sides of each third piece.
13. Arrange six of these thirds around the large cane to form another layer of petals and gently press the stack together.
14. Flatten the last six thirds even more than the previous ones and arrange these around the large cane to form the last layer of petals.
15. Roll a quarter of a block of translucent clay through the pasta machine on setting 1. Cut the strip to match the width of the flower cane. Wrap the cane in the strip of clay, as you would when you are making a bull's eye cane.
16. Reduce the cane slightly, working from the middle, to get rid of all the air bubbles.
17. Wrap the cane in another strip of translucent clay to complete the abstract flower cane.

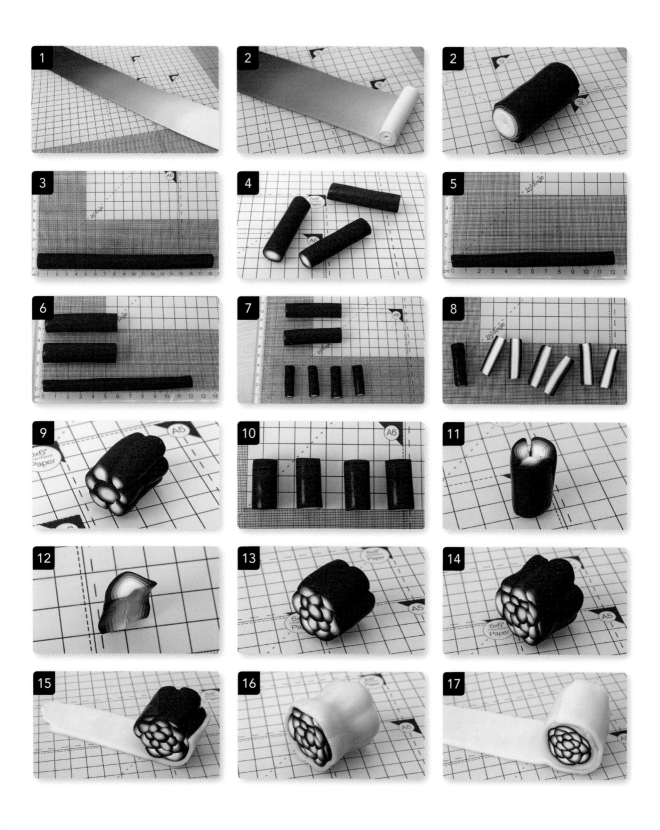

Orange and blue flower cane

1. Use half a block each of white and orange clay to make a blended cane (Skinner's technique). Begin rolling at the white end of the sheet to provide a white centre. Reduce the cane to measure 10 cm in length.
2. Cut the cane into five equal segments measuring 2 cm each.
3. Pinch both sides of each cane to resemble an eye.
4. Shape two of the canes into half-moons, place them on either side of the eye-shaped canes, and gently press them together.
5. Press the remaining two canes to either side of the centre cane.
6. Roll and reduce the cane to measure approximately 4 cm.
7. Run a quarter of a brown block of clay through the pasta machine on setting 1 and cut it to match the size of the orange cane.
8. Wrap the orange cane in the brown clay, as you would when making a bull's eye cane.
9. Reduce the cane to measure 12 cm after the ends have been trimmed neatly.
10. Divide the cane into six even segments measuring 2 cm each.
11. Make a bull's eye cane using a white and brown Skinner blend that is wrapped in a layer of light blue clay. I didn't make the cane specifically for this project; it's a left-over bit from another project. You can use any other colours for the centre of the flower. If you don't have any leftover bits of bull's eye canes, you don't have to make a blended sheet especially for this project. You need very little clay for the centre.
12. Shape petals using the six brown and orange canes and arrange them around the bull's eye cane.
13. Roll a quarter block of light blue clay through the pasta machine on setting 1. Roll little snakes using some of the light blue clay and press these into the gaps between the petals.
14. Cut the rest of the blue clay to match the width of the flower cane. Wrap the cane, as you would when you are making a bull's eye cane.
15. Reduce to form a flower cane should you wish to use it for a specific project.

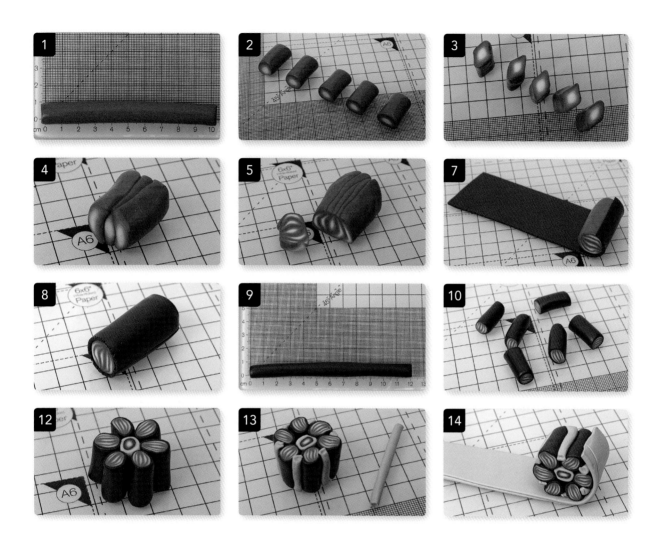

Double petal flower cane

1. Make a blended cane (Skinner's technique) using half a block each of dark pink and white clay. The outer layer must be pink and the centre white.
2. Cut the cane in half lengthwise.
3. Use a wooden stick or any long, round object that measures 5 mm in diameter, and press one half of the cane around the object. The white must be on the inside and the sides of the cane should nearly meet.
4. Carefully remove the stick or object.
5. Use a left-over bit of black clay to roll a snake and press it into the indentation left by the round object. Wrap the pink ends around the black clay, but do not allow the pink ends to meet.
6. Fold and shape the other half of the original cane around the cane that you have just shaped.
7. Cut the cane in half to form two petals.
8. Press the petals together.
9. Reduce the cane to measure 12 cm.
10. Divide the cane into six equal pieces measuring 2 cm each.
11. Arrange the petals to form one large flower and determine the size of the centre.
12. Roll a piece of black clay until it is thin enough to fit into the centre and assemble the petals around it. Press the pieces together firmly.
13. Reduce the cane, but separate the petals regularly by inserting a blade between them.
14. Also try other colour variations.

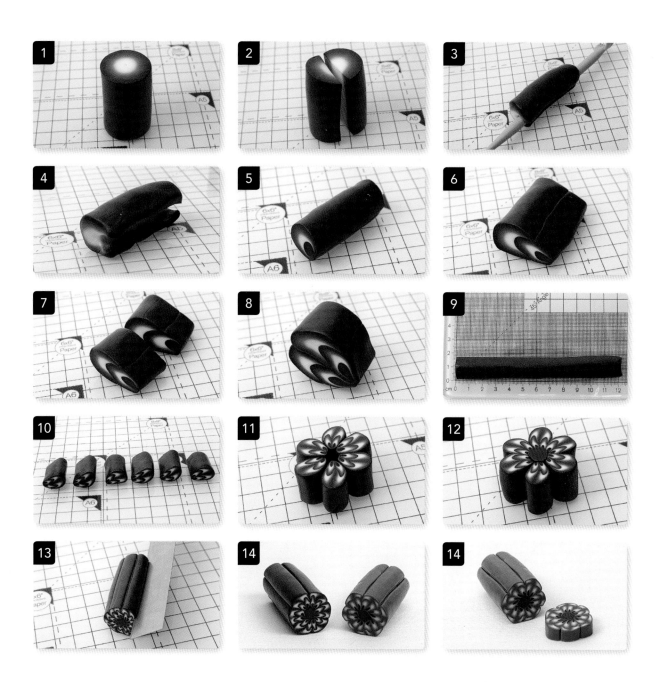

Black-and-white flower millefiori

1. Use half a block of white clay to roll a log that is 5 cm long and 2,5 cm in diameter.
2. Use a flexible blade and cut the log into lengths as indicated.
3. Roll half a block of black clay through the pasta machine on setting 1. Cut out a square that is large enough to cover one side of the larger log.
4. Cut the remaining, smaller white log in half lengthwise.
5. Insert a strip of black clay between the halves, but it must not extend right through the centre.
6. Reassemble the two halves of the original log.
7. Roll a snake of black clay and press it onto the white log as indicated.
8. Wrap the remaining black clay around the white log until it touches the black snake, as indicated.
9. Reduce the cane to a length of 24 cm, taking care to maintain the shape of the petal.
10. Divide the cane into eight equal pieces measuring 3 cm each.
11. Arrange the eight petals to form a circle and determine the size of the centre.
12. Make a bull's eye cane using the remaining white and black clay. Use black for the centre with a layer of white and black around it. Place the bull's eye cane between the petals and press together firmly.
13. Condition half a block of translucent clay and roll it through the pasta machine on setting 1. Roll a little piece of the clay into snakes to insert between the petals.
14. Complete the flower cane using the rest of the translucent clay to form a double layer around the cane (as you would when making a bull's eye cane).

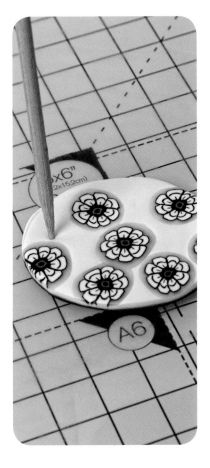

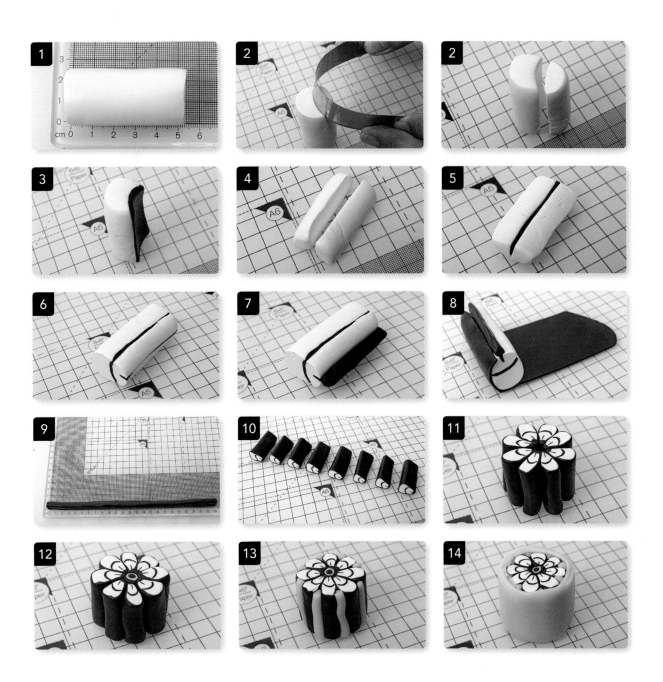

Purple and orange flower cane

1. Use one block each of purple, white, and orange clay to make a blended cane (using Skinner's technique). Place the white clay between the purple and orange. Make sure that you have a really long strip by rolling it through the pasta machine on setting 3.

2. Fold the strip of clay from the orange to the purple side using a fan fold.

3. Press the folds firmly together and cut the clay stack into an uneven number of strips. I used nine strips.

4. Reassemble the strips so that the different colours form steps.

5. Cut the bottom half from the clay stack, neatly halving the centre strip (of the nine).

6. Insert the cut section into the top half and press together firmly.

7. Reduce the block to a length of 15 cm.

8. Divide each square cane into five equal parts measuring 3 cm each.

9. Assemble five parts to form a cube.

10. Press the sides of the cube together to form a log or round cane.

11. Cut a strip from the remaining purple clay and wrap it around the orange and purple clay as you would when making a bull's eye cane.

12. Reduce the cane to a length of 18 cm.

13. Cut it into six equal pieces measuring 6 cm each.

14. Make a bull's eye cane using purple and orange clay. Pinch each of the six pieces into a petal shape and arrange the pieces around the bull's eye cane.

15. Roll half a block of translucent clay through the pasta machine on setting 1. Roll little snakes and insert these between the petals.

16. Wrap a double layer of translucent clay around the flower cane, as you would when you are making a bull's eye cane.

17. Reduce the flower cane when you need to use it for a specific project.

18. Other colour combinations for this specific cane can also be very striking.

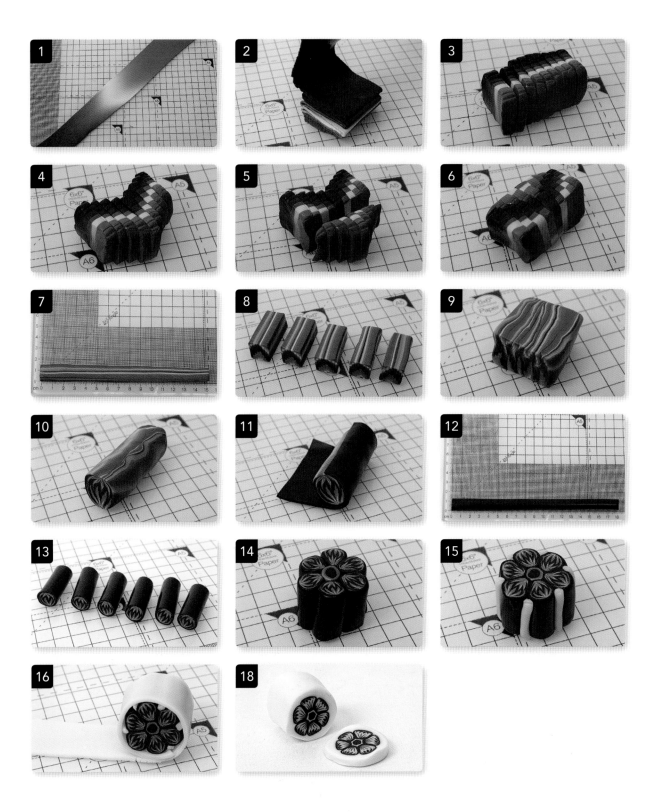

Classy coasters

These coasters are really quick to make and, because you really can't go wrong, they are ideal if you need to make a special gift in a jiffy. The example was created using black clay on wood coasters. They also look stunning if you use glass coasters and white instead of black clay.

MATERIAL AND TOOLS

½ block of clay per coaster

Variety of objects to texture the clay

Pigment powder in the colour of your choice

Liquid polymer clay or craft glue

Sosatie (kebab) skewers

Pasta machine or roller

Soft paintbrush

Blades

Wood or glass coasters

METHOD

1. Condition the clay and roll it through the pasta machine on setting 1. If you don't have a pasta machine, use a stack of six playing cards on either side of the clay that you are rolling out to ensure a consistent thickness. Cut out a neat square or rectangle.

2. Firmly press the objects, such as pen covers, chains, jewellery findings, and even screwdrivers, into the clay to texture it.

3. Cover the entire square in impressions.

4. Cut the clay square into squares and rectangles of various sizes.

5. Spray liquid polymer clay onto the coaster.

6. Spread the clay over small sections of the coaster using a skewer. As you proceed, you will have to apply more liquid clay. The coating of liquid clay must be very thin. You can also use craft glue, but it has to be applied sparingly.

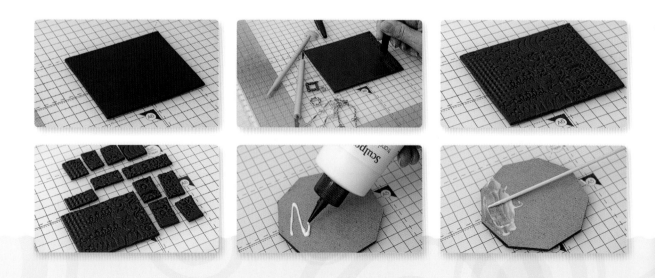

7. Position the little square and rectangular clay tiles on the coaster and neatly trim the edges.

8. Repeat until the entire coaster is covered by clay tiles. Be sure to finish the edges neatly.

9. Brush pigment powder over the surface of the clay, using a soft paintbrush. The colour of the pigment powder is very intense. Be careful not to apply too much powder. You can use one colour or a few colours.

10. Cover the entire surface of the coaster in pigment powder. If you are not satisfied with the result, wipe off some of the powder using a wet cloth. However, this is not recommended.

11. Bake the coaster according to the clay manufacturer's instructions.

12. Experiment with various colour combinations.

Clay-decorated clay pots

I bought these little clay pots many years ago, knowing that I would be able to put them to good, creative use someday. Small succulent plants look beautiful in these little pots and together they form an interesting focal point.

MATERIAL AND TOOLS

Small clay pots (or any other pot-plant container that can resist oven temperatures of 130 °C)

½ block each of green, yellow, red and brown clay

Offcuts of white clay

Flower cookie cutter

Liquid polymer clay

Pasta machine or roller

Blades

Rubber gloves

METHOD

1. Roll the clay that you are going to use to cover the pot through the pasta machine on setting 3. If you are using playing cards, use a stack of three cards. Cut a small strip to cover the rim of the pot.

2. Apply liquid polymer clay to the rim. You must cover it before you start covering the rest of the pot.

3. Press the clay strip into place along the rim. Wear rubber gloves so as not to leave fingerprints on the clay.

4. Neatly trim the strip of clay where the ends meet.

5. Trim the clay along the top (ridge).

6. Also trim the clay neatly just below the rim.

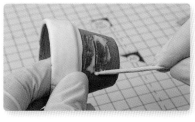

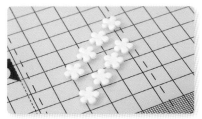

7. Apply liquid polymer clay to the rest of the pot (lower section).

8. Cut a strip of clay broad enough to cover this section and firmly press it onto the pot. Try to press it neatly around the edges.

9. Trim the clay along the bottom edge.

10. Repeat the steps for all the pots and colours that you will be using, and bake the pots in the oven according to the clay manufacturer's instructions.

11. Roll the offcuts of white and yellow clay through the pasta machine on setting 3. Use the cookie cutter to cut out a number of flowers.

12. Apply a drop of liquid polymer clay to the spots where you want to place the flowers, and attach them.

13. Roll tiny balls of yellow clay to use as centres for the white flowers, and attach them.

14. Make yellow flowers with white centres for the red pot.

15. Roll tiny balls of white, yellow and red balls to decorate the rim of the brown pot.

16. Decorate the yellow pot with a red bow.

17. After you have decorated the pots, they must be baked again to cure the decorations.

Soap dish

Some hand basins don't have a spot to put the soap. As a result, the soap ends up in the water and soon becomes soft and slippery. Making a soap dish according to your taste is the solution. This soap dish is ready for use in a jiffy.

MATERIALS AND TOOLS

2 blocks of clay: 1 grey granite, 1 white granite

A shape to cut the clay

Pasta machine or roller

Blades

Sosatie (kebab) skewers

METHOD

1. Condition the clay well and roll both colours through the pasta machine on setting 1. Cut out the shape of the soap dish from both colours.

2. Place the two colours on top of each other and lightly run your fingers over the surface of the clay to force out any air bubbles.

3. Use a skewer or any other sharp object to pierce the centre of the clay shape. This will ensure that the soap does not lie in water.

4. Use the remaining grey clay to roll a log that is 4 cm long and 1,5 cm in diameter.

5. Cut the log into four equal pieces to shape the props of the dish.

6. Press the props onto the bottom of the dish, taking care to position them equally far from the corners.

7. Shape the dish to ensure that the water will drain towards the centre.

8. Bake the soap dish according the clay manufacturer's instructions.

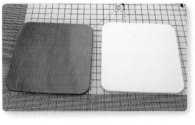

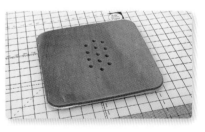

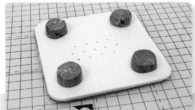
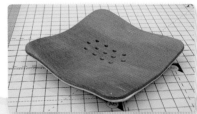

Elegant rose photo frame

Photos are proudly displayed, one way or another, in most homes. Nowadays, the popular trend is to use a variety of frames and present them as a collection. Why not make this elegant frame to add to your collection?

MATERIAL AND TOOLS

Wooden frame

White craft paint

Large paintbrush

½ block pearlescent clay

½ block white clay

Pasta machine or roller

Extruder or clay gun (optional)

Craft glue or liquid polymer clay

Blades

METHOD

1. Condition the clay and mix the white and pearlescent clay thoroughly.

2. Roll the clay through the pasta machine on setting 4. Shape clay roses as described on p. 21. I made one large rose, five medium-sized and seven small roses. I also made five rose buds (with only three petals). Bake the roses according to the clay manufacturer's instructions.

3. Paint the wooden frame white. It must have a lime-washed finish.

4. Use the extruder (clay gun) to extrude a neat, even strip of clay, or roll a clay cord by hand. Be sure to roll the cord evenly. Attach this cord to the inner and outer edges of the photo frame, using liquid polymer clay or craft glue.

5. Use craft glue to attach the roses to two sides of the photo frame. Start by placing the largest rose in the top, left-hand corner of the frame, followed by the medium and smaller roses, and the rose buds.

6. Bake the frame, with roses and cord attached, to cure the cord.

Stringed photo frame

This simple, striped frame is really striking precisely because of its simplicity. It is also very easy to make. Unfortunately, you are going to find it difficult to make if you don't have a clay gun.

MATERIAL AND TOOLS

Wooden frame
½ block pearlescent clay
½ block white clay
½ block gold clay
Extruder (clay gun)
Liquid polymer clay
Blade

METHOD

1. Condition the clay and make the gold clay a shade lighter by mixing it with half of the white clay.

2. Roll even-sized logs (measuring approximately 2 cm) from the white, gold and pearlescent clay and insert these into the barrel of the extruder (clay gun).

3. Use the die that has 12 holes and extrude the clay.

4. The strips of clay will contain various gradations of white, gold and pearlescent.

5. Apply liquid polymer clay to the edges of the photo frame. Carefully attach the strips to the frame. Be patient and work neatly and precisely.

6. Once the entire frame has been covered, use a blade to neatly trim the strips along the edges of the frame.

7. Also trim the inside edge of the frame neatly.

8. Bake the frame in the oven, following the clay manufacturer's baking instructions.

Tiny work of art on canvas

When you mix two or more colours of polymer clay, the result is often a surprise – and you will never achieve identical effects. You may try to use paint to create a similar work of art, but clay has a certain charm that cannot be captured with a paintbrush.

MATERIAL AND TOOLS

½ block each of black, white and turquoise clay

13 cm x 18 cm canvas

Pasta machine or roller

Blades

Double-sided tape

Extra-thick embossing enamel (UTEE)

Heat gun

Liquid polymer clay

Paintbrush

Two square sponges of different sizes (3,5 cm x 3,5 cm and 1,5 cm x 1,5 cm)

Flower punch

METHOD

1. Condition the clay well and mix these combinations: white and turquoise; and white, black and turquoise. In order to enhance the marble effect, the colours should not be mixed excessively.

2. Run the clay through the pasta machine on setting 5. The sheets will be paper-thin.

3. Use the heat gun to cure the thin sheets of clay.

4. When the clay sheets have cured and cooled, punch five large squares, four small squares, and one flower from the clay. Try to obtain various shades of colours for each of the squares.

5. Brush liquid polymer clay onto one square and sprinkle over some embossing enamel powder.

6. Use the heat gun to melt the embossing enamel.

7. Sprinkle another layer of the embossing powder over the square and heat immediately using the heat gun.

8. Repeat at least three more times. After the third layer of embossing enamel has been added, it will look as if resin has been cast over the clay.

9. Roll white clay through the pasta machine on setting 1 and cut squares to match the sizes of the punched squares. Coat the white surfaces with liquid polymer clay and press the turquoise and blue squares firmly onto the white squares.

10. Bake the clay according to the clay manufacturer's instructions and allow it to cool.

11. Arrange the squares on the canvas according to your taste, and attach them with double-sided tape.

Button carnival

I had such fun while making these buttons! Buttons can be functional or decorative – or both. When making buttons for an item of clothing, you have to bear the following in mind. The buttons are machine washable, provided that the temperature of the water is not too high. Never tumble-dry clothing that has polymer clay buttons.

MATERIALS AND TOOLS

Clay – various colours
Cookie cutters
Pasta machine or roller
Blades
Toothpicks to pierce the clay
Tons of imagination and creativity

METHOD

I really cannot provide a specific method! Just use your own methods and, hopefully, you will enjoy the experience as much as I did.

- The possibilities are endless. You can play around to your heart's content, and each button will be unique.
- Use cookie cutters to produce a variety of shapes.
- Mix your own colours so that the buttons match specific outfits.
- Make buttons according to specific themes, for example use an anchor for a naval theme, or hearts to represent love.
- Use slices of any of the canes described on pages 24 to 51 and simply pierce them to turn them into buttons.
- Use the buttons to make a necklace with a difference …
- or to decorate photo frames.

- Use buttons on scatter cushions to change their appearance completely …

- or on satchels or laptop bags for a cool, playful finish …

- Because the buttons are made of baked and cured clay, you can also use them on placemats or heatproof trivets to be used for hot dishes.

- Give the buttons to children to create pictures …

- or jazz up their hair clips and Alice-bands.

- See how many uses you can add to this list.

Decorated candle

A snow-white candle always looks stylish, and these white and silver clay decorations will add extra-special charm. The decorations are quick and easy to make, and you can produce a beautiful candle for you dinner table, or for Christmas, in no time at all.

MATERIALS AND TOOLS

Any white candle

¼ block white clay

Silver glitter glue

1 x 6 mm silver-grey pearl

2 x 4 mm silver-grey pearls

13 x sterling silver headpins with ball points

Pasta machine or roller

Craft knife with fine point

Flower cookie cutters (2 different sizes)

METHOD

1. Roll the white clay through the pasta machine on setting 2 and cover the sheet in cling film.

2. Use the cookie cutter to cut out one large and two smaller flowers. The cling film ensures that the edges of the flowers are slightly rounded.

3. Use the craft knife to texture the flowers.

4. Create a border by using glitter glue around the edges of the flowers.

5. Make a few dots on the petals.

6. Use the cookie cutter to cut out several small flowers.

7. Pierce the centres of all the flowers.

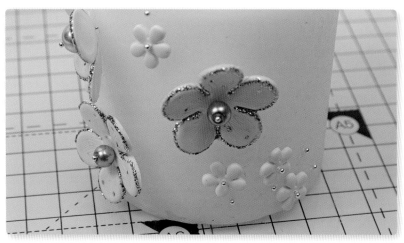

8. Bake all the flowers according to the clay manufacturer's instructions. Bake the large and medium flowers on glass balls to shape them so that they are not completely flat.

9. Thread the pearls and flowers onto the headpins as indicated. The 6-mm pearl is used with the larger flowers, and the 4-mm pearls with the smaller flowers. The tiniest flowers must be threaded separately.

10. Press the flowers with the silver edges into the candle.

11. Then press the smaller flower into the candle as well; and use the headpins on their own to add the finishing touches.

Decorated teaspoons

Follow these easy steps to make an exceptional gift for someone special.
A set of teaspoons and cake forks also make for a welcome and practical gift.

MATERIALS AND TOOLS

Teaspoons – as many as you
wish to cover

Black and white clay (you can cover
4 – 6 teaspoons with 1 block of clay)

Pasta machine or roller

Liquid polymer clay

Blades

Rubber gloves

METHOD

1. Roll black clay through the pasta machine on setting 4. Make sure that the sheet of clay is large enough to cover the spoon.

2. Use a jelly cane made of black and white clay and cut thin slices from it. Arrange the slices on the sheet of black clay.

3. Use a roller to flatten the slices on the black clay sheet.

4. Repeat the steps for the second and third spoon, but use thin slices of another cane to arrange on the black clay.

5. Apply a very thin coat of liquid polymer clay to the spoon.

6. Place the decorated sheet of black clay on the spoon.

7. Wear rubber gloves, so as not to leave fingerprints in the clay, and press the clay onto the front of the spoon. Make sure that all the air is forced out.

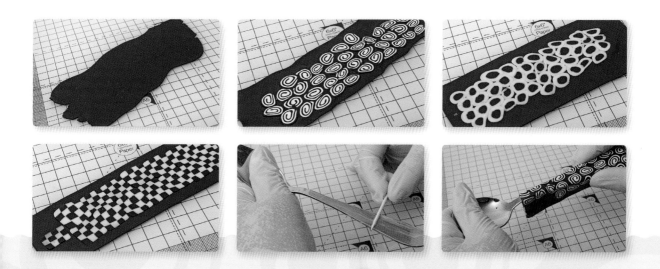

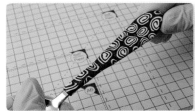

8. Turn the spoon around and press the clay onto the spoon, working from the front to the back. Start pressing the clay onto the spoon from the left side, and trim excess clay using a small, sharp blade.

9. Bring the clay around from the right side to the back, and carefully trim the excess clay so that the ends meet neatly.

10. Smooth out the clay around the entire spoon and neaten the end of the spoon.

11. Repeat the steps for each spoon.

Retro cutlery

The trend nowadays is to set the table using different dinnerware for each place setting to create a cosy, informal atmosphere. I used a retro cane to cover this cutlery. You can use a different colour for each set, and then mix all the colours for a delightful, multi-coloured table. You can also make serviette rings in various colours.

MATERIALS AND TOOLS

1 knife, 1 fork, 1 dessert spoon and 1 teaspoon per set

Retro cane (See p. 36)

½ block clay in a colour that matches the retro cane

Pasta machine or roller

Blades

A round object, such as a glass bottle, to shape the serviette ring

METHOD

1. Prepare clay and follow steps to cover cutlery, described on p. 73.

2. Cover one set using the same retro cane, and use other colours for the next set. (See colour combinations used for retro canes on p. 36.)

3. Make the serviette ring:

   • Run the matching clay through the pasta machine on setting 1.

   • Cut thin slices from the retro cane and arrange on the clay strip.

   • Roll decorated strip through the pasta machine.

4. Measure the circumference of the shape that you are going to use to bake the serviette ring. The circumference of the bottle that I used is 11 cm. Cut a neat strip measuring 3 cm x the circumference (11 cm).

5. Carefully wrap the strip around the bottle.

6. Brush liquid polymer clay over the butt joint for a neat, secure finish. The liquid polymer clay becomes translucent once cured.

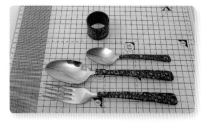

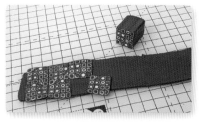

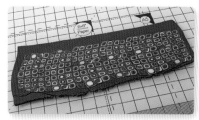

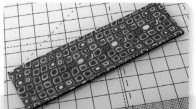

Mirror for a little princess

You can create the most amazing mosaic tiles using polymer clay. Because it is so much lighter than glass, even large projects will remain nice and light. For this project, I made paper-thin tiles using a punch to ensure that they were all the same size. The tiles are so thin, you can even use a pair of scissors to cut them into various shapes if you wish. I didn't use grout between the tiles – the layer of clay under the tiles serves this purpose.

MATERIALS AND TOOLS

Flat block of wood 13 cm x 13 cm

Small, square mirror 8 cm x 8 cm

½ block each: pink, purple and white clay

Heat gun

Enough offcut bits of clay in a light colour to make a frame for the mirror

Pastamachine or roller

Liquid polymer clay

Square punch

Flower and heart punch

Glitter powder

Craft glue

Blades

Craft knife

METHOD

1. Condition the clay, and mix the pink, purple and white using various combinations to create different marbled blends. Roll out the clay very thinly – using setting 5 on the pasta machine. Place the sheets on a tile and cure the clay using a heat gun.

2. Once the clay has cured and cooled, punch at least 20 little squares, and a few hearts and flowers from the clay. Set the tiles aside for later use.

3. Roll the offcuts through the pasta machine on setting 1.

4. Place the mirror in the centre of the block of wood and mark the position using a pencil.

5. Apply liquid polymer clay to the sections of the wood not covered by the mirror.

6. Place the offcut sheet of clay on the wood and firmly press it into position.

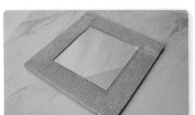

7. Place the mirror on the clay and, using a craft knife, cut out the section where the mirror will be placed. Neatly trim the clay around the edges.

8. Bake the clay-covered frame according to the clay manufacturer's instructions.

9. When the frame is cured and cooled, apply liquid polymer clay to the section where the mirror is to be fixed, and position the mirror.

10. Apply liquid polymer clay to the border around the mirror.

11. Sprinkle glitter powder onto the liquid polymer clay.

12. Do this around the entire border.

13. Heat the area, using a heat gun, to cure the liquid polymer clay and to ensure that the glitter sticks.

14. Use craft glue to paste the square tiles onto the frame and paste a flower and a heart alternately on every second tile.

Keyring and bracelet

The keyring and bracelet made of glow-in-the-dark clay will also be luminous. Both are made using scraps of clay and they are easy to string.

MATERIALS AND TOOLS

Scraps of glow-in-the-dark clay and black clay (left-overs from the mobile on p. 82)

Keyring

Pasta machine or roller

15 black glass beads

Fishing line

20 cm elastic

METHOD

1. Condition the clay and roll it through the pasta machine on setting 1.

2. Make a bull's eye cane with a glow-in-the-dark centre covered in black clay. Cut beads measuring 1 cm and pierce them.

3. Cut out three circles from the glow-in-the-dark clay and stack them, firmly pressing them together.

4. Use the black clay to make a smiley face on each of the circles. Pierce the circle along its length.

5. Make four small beads and another smiley face.

6. Mix all the scraps of clay (black and glow-in-the-dark) and make round beads. Pierce them.

7. Bake all the objects according to the clay manufacturer's instructions.

8. Once the clay has cured and cooled, make the keyring and bracelet as indicated.

Luminous mobile

Clay that glows in the dark can be used to entertain your child once the light in the bedroom has been switched off at night. The clay will glow for quite some time – quite possibly until the child falls asleep. You can use a few stars and moons to create the mobile, or simply paste clay shapes here, there and everywhere in the bedroom.

MATERIALS AND TOOLS

2 blocks of glow-in-the-dark clay

¼ block black clay

Cookie cutters: star, crescent moon, circle

Pasta machine or roller

Short wooden rod

Fishing line

Crimp beads

METHOD

1. Condition the glow-in-the-dark clay and roll it through the pasta machine on setting 1.

2. Cut out six small and two large stars, and two moons.

3. Make five round clay beads.

4. Pierce the beads, and the top and the bottom of each clay shape. Bake the clay according to the clay manufacturer's instructions. Be careful not to bake the clay for too long since it darkens easily.

5. Make notches in the middle and at each end of the rod where the strings of star and moon shapes will be attached. Assemble the mobile as follows:

- Thread fishing line through a star or moon, followed by a crimp bead and a clay bead, and then another star or moon. Make a loop and close the crimp bead to ensure that the shapes remain together.

- Make two strings using the following combination: small star, bead, moon, bead, small star.

- Make one string using: a small star, bead, large star, bead, small star, bead, and another large star.

- Attach the strings to the rod and make a loop from which to suspend the mobile.

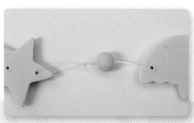

Brightly coloured keyrings

I often present craft classes for children and keyrings are always popular projects. They are easy enough to make, and the children have a cute gift to take home. I usually give each child two quarter blocks of clay in different colours. They soon team up and exchange pieces of clay so they normally end up having more than two colours to work with.

MATERIALS AND TOOLS

Small pieces of clay of various colours (½ block in total)

Keyring

A variety of findings

Stringing material

METHOD

1. Make beads of various shapes and sizes using the clay you have available.

2. Pierce the beads – the holes must be large enough for the stringing material to be doubled – and bake them according to the clay manufacturer's instructions.

3. Knot the stringing material to fix it to the keyring as indicated.

4. Thread the beads and findings either following a pattern or simply randomly.

5. Once all the beads and findings have been threaded, press them up against the ring to ensure that there are no gaps between them. Make a double knot at the end of the last silver finding.

6. Tie the two strings.

7. Cover the knot with clear nail polish and trim the ends.

Notebook and business card holders

This set will make a unique gift for someone special. You can personalise it by imprinting the receiver's name in the clay before it is baked. I used a notebook with a screw-on, aluminium front cover. Use anything that can withstand the temperature at which the clay will be baked.

MATERIALS AND TOOLS

Wooden business card holder

Black craft paint

Paintbrush

Notebook holder

1 block black clay

Rubber letter stamps

Pigment powder

Round cookie cutter

Liquid polymer clay

Brain cane (see p. 37)

Pasta machine or roller

Rubber gloves

Blades

Dressmaker's tracing wheel

Steel ruler

METHOD

1. Paint the business card holder black and allow the paint to dry thoroughly.

2. Condition the black clay and roll it through the pasta machine on setting 4. Set aside a little piece of clay for the nametag.

3. Cut very thin slices from the brain cane and arrange them on the black clay.

4. Use a roller to flatten the slices or run the clay through the pasta machine again. The sheet must be big enough to cover the front of the notebook as well as the business card holder.

5. Apply liquid polymer clay to the aluminium cover of the notebook holder.

6. Wearing rubber gloves, press the patterned sheet of clay onto the cover. Use a sharp blade to trim the clay around the edges.

7. Repeat steps 5 and 6 to make the front cover of the business card holder.

8. Roll the black clay reserved for the nametag through the pasta machine on setting 2. Carefully trim the edges.

9. Use the tracing wheel to create a neat border in the trimmed black clay.

10. Use rubber stamps to imprint the name in the clay. Use the ruler to keep the letters in a straight line.

11. Use the tracing wheel to underline the name.

12. Lightly rub pigment powder into the letters. Use the powder sparingly – the colours are very bright.

13. Cut a slice from the brain cane to decorate the top of the business card holder, and attach it in the centre using liquid polymer clay.

14. Cure the notebook cover and the business card holder in the oven, following the clay manufacturer's instructions.

Calligraphy box

I 'dressed' the wooden box in which I keep all my calligraphy pens in a new clay 'jacket' and I am really impressed with the final product. I was newly inspired to take up my pens and write! Decorate any memory box according to your taste.

MATERIALS AND TOOLS

Wooden box – any size

Clay in shades of brown, bronze, orange, and green (jointly 2 full blocks)

Rubber or acrylic stamps

Liquid polymer clay

Pasta machine or roller

Sosatie (kebab) skewer

Rubber gloves

Blades

Paintbrush

Heat gun

METHOD

1. Condition half a block of brown clay and roll it through the pasta machine on setting 4. Cut a long, thin strip that will fit around the edges of the lid.

2. Apply liquid polymer clay to one of the long edges of the lid.

3. Wearing rubber gloves, press the clay firmly onto the edge.

4. Use a sosatie (kebab) skewer to shape the rounded edges neatly.

5. Carefully trim the excess clay along the bottom.

6. Repeat these steps to cover the two short sides and the other long side of the lid, as well as the four sides of the box. Cure in the oven according to the clay manufacturer's instructions.

7. Plan the lid cover before you start cutting the clay and decorating the box. Measure it and decide into how many parts you want to divide it, and how each part will be decorated. This is merely a suggestion. Whatever you decide to do, just make sure that your measurements are accurate.

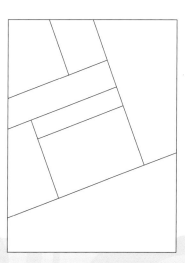

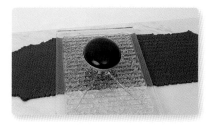
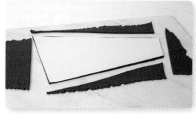

8. Cut out paper patterns according to your planning.

9. Place the clay on a tile; to ensure that the various parts will fit precisely, the clay should not be lifted off the tile until it has cured.

10. Roll brown clay through the pasta machine on setting 3. Firmly press the word stamp into the clay.

11. Place the paper pattern on the clay according to your planning, and cut it accordingly.

12. Mix the different colours of clay to achieve various marbled effects, and cut all the sections according to your planning. You can use rubber stamps on more than one section.

13. Bake the clay on the tile, following the clay manufacturer's instruction, and allow it to cool.

14. Apply liquid polymer clay over the entire lid.

15. Press the different pieces of clay into position on the lid.

16. Proceed as follows for the writing. Print the words or text on ordinary, or special, paper. Position the words according to your planning. Apply liquid polymer clay to the section(s) that will be covered in writing.

17. Spread the liquid polymer clay evenly. The layer of liquid clay must be the same height as the surrounding clay areas.

18. Bake the entire lid in the oven, according to the clay manufacturer's instructions. The liquid polymer clay becomes slightly translucent.

19. Use the heat gun to make the liquid polymer clay completely translucent.

Notebook with the appearance of leather

A large notebook for big ideas! This stunning cover will definitely inspire you to write down your creative ideas without delay – before they can be forgotten.

MATERIALS AND TOOLS

Notebook with hard cover

2 blocks of clay – brown and turquoise

Pasta machine and roller

Craft glue

Dressmaker's tracing wheel

Raffia

Flower stamp

Brown acrylic paint

Blades

Heat gun

METHOD

1. Condition the clay and roll it through the pasta machine on setting 2.

2. Roll raffia over the brown clay to give it a leathery texture.

3. Repeat until you are satisfied with the result.

4. Press the flower stamp firmly into the turquoise clay.

5. Repeat until the pattern pleases you.

6. Cut paper patterns according to the size of the book, and cut the clay to match the patterns.

7. To create the appearance of stitching, place a leftover bit of turquoise clay on the edge of the brown clay. Use the tracing wheel to roll a straight line along the edge through the turquoise clay. If you want to keep the line straight, use a ruler.

8. Remove turquoise clay to reveal the 'stitching' on the brown clay.

9. Lightly apply brown, acrylic paint over the turquoise to accentuate the flower pattern.

10. Carefully wipe off any excess paint using a dry cloth.

11. Use the heat gun to dry the paint completely.

12. Use an earbud to remove excess paint from between the flowers.

13. Bake the clay on the tile, following the clay manufacturer's instructions. Allow the clay to cool and paste it onto the notebook using craft glue.

Cheerful pencil case and paperclips

If you make this brightly coloured pencil case for one of your children, it will definitely be the only one of its kind in class! Use bright, neon clay for a jolly explosion of colour.

MATERIALS AND TOOLS

Pencil case – any size

3 x extra large paperclips

Enough brightly coloured scraps of clay to cover the case

1 block white clay

Mosaic cane (see p. 34)

Round cookie cutter

Pasta machine or roller

Liquid polymer clay

Rubber gloves

Blades

METHOD

1. Condition the scraps of clay by rolling the bits through the pasta machine on setting 4.

2. Apply a very thin coat of liquid polymer clay to the case. Only the lid must be covered.

3. Wearing rubber gloves, press the clay firmly onto the surface of the case. Make sure that all the air is forced out.

4. Neatly trim the clay around the edges of the lid.

5. Cure the clay in the oven, following the clay manufacturer's instructions, and allow it to cool.

6. In the meantime, roll the white clay through the pasta machine on setting 4. Cut very thin slices from the mosaic cane and arrange them on the white clay. Roll the sheet through the pasta machine again.

7. Some sections contain smaller tiles; this is because I reduced the mosaic cane further before cutting off these slices.

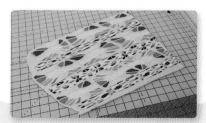
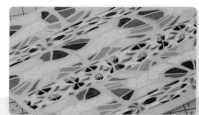

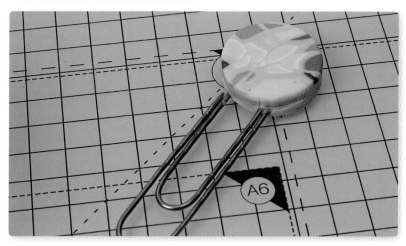

8. Cover the lid with the mosaic sheet using the method described for the sheet of scrap clay, and bake again according to the clay manufacturer's instructions. Keep any leftover bits of the mosaic sheet.

9. Make the paperclips by rolling the same scraps of clay that were used for the pencil case through the pasta machine on setting 1. Use a cookie cutter to cut out circles from this sheet of clay as well as from the leftover mosaic sheet.

10. Liberally apply liquid polymer clay to the scrap sheet circles and firmly press them onto the paperclips. Apply liquid polymer clay to the paperclips as well.

11. Place the mosaic circle on top of the scrap sheet circle on the paperclip, and press it firmly into position.

12. Bake according to the clay manufacturer's instructions.

String of rainbow beads

I found the striking, bright colours of this clay alluring. This long string of beads would look gorgeous worn with a white or pastel outfit. Shades of black, grey, and white would look very smart, while earthy colours would look natural. Rope as stringing material is a good choice when you are using earthy colours.

MATERIALS AND TOOLS

Scraps of clay – approximately 1 block in total

½ block each of the following colours: neon orange, bright pink, purple, neon green, bright yellow, white

20 small bead caps

20 larger bead caps

20 eye pins

1 m silver chain

Extruder (clay gun)

Piercing tool (awl)

Flat-nose pliers

METHOD

1. Make 10 large, round beads using the scraps of clay. To ensure that the beads are all the same size, roll the clay into a log and then cut off even-sized pieces before you start rolling the beads. My log was 1 cm in diameter and I divided it into 2-cm pieces.

2. Pierce the beads using a piercing tool.

3. Mix ¼ block of each of the bright colours with ⅛ block white clay to create a marbled effect. Roll each of the clay mixes into a log that is 1,5 cm long.

4. Press the logs together.

5. Place the plug of clay into the barrel of the extruder (clay gun).

6. Insert the die containing 12 round holes into the gun and extrude the clay. Thin strips of clay will be extruded.

7. The colour of the strips will gradually change from one hue to another.

8. Carefully wrap strips of multi-coloured clay around each bead. Be patient and try to work precisely.

9. Cover the entire bead. If the string of clay is too short, join it with the next as inconspicuously as possible.

10. Make two, small, round beads of each colour.

11. Thread the beads onto the metal pins of the baking rack. If you don't have a baking rack, an oven pan can be used. Cover the base of the pan with a layer of Maizena, and then bake the beads in it.

12. Bake all the beads, following the clay manufacturer's instructions, and allow them to cool. Thread a large bead cap, rainbow bead and another bead cap onto a long eyepin.

13. Use the round-nose pliers to make an eyelet at the end of the eyepin.

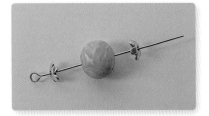

14. Thread a small bead cap, small bead and another bead cap onto an eyepin.

15. Make an eyelet on the other end of the eyepin, and attach a 5-cm piece of the silver chain to both sides of the small beads.

16. Attach a rainbow bead to each end of the chain.

17. Alternate the colours of the small beads, and repeat these steps until all the beads form one, long chain.

Chunky but light

Because polymer clay is available in such beautiful, vibrant colours, it is only natural that one would have the urge to create something chunky and colourful. However, chunky clay beads are quite heavy. In order to solve this problem, you can use light, wooden beads and wrap them in clay.

MATERIALS AND TOOLS

Jelly cane with three colours (see p. 28) – approximately 2 cm

Bull's eye cane (see p. 25) – approximately 2 cm

Striped cane (see p. 30) – approximately 2 cm

Lace cane (see p. 27) – approximately 2 cm

1 large wooden bead as the focal bead

2 slightly smaller wooden beads

6 medium-sized wooden beads

22 small wooden beads

½ block orange clay

38 bronze flower spacers

Bronze clasp

1 m cord

2 crimp beads

Varnish

Liquid polymer clay

Paintbrush

METHOD

1. Apply liquid polymer clay to the largest bead and cover it using thin slices of the jelly cane.

2. Cover two medium-sized beads using slices of the lace cane.

3. Cover another two using slices of the bull's eye cane.

4. Cover the remaining two medium-sized beads using slices of the black-and-white striped cane.

5. Insert the orange clay into the clay gun and extrude thin strips.

6. Apply liquid polymer clay to the two second largest wooden beads, and carefully attach strips of extruded clay to each bead.

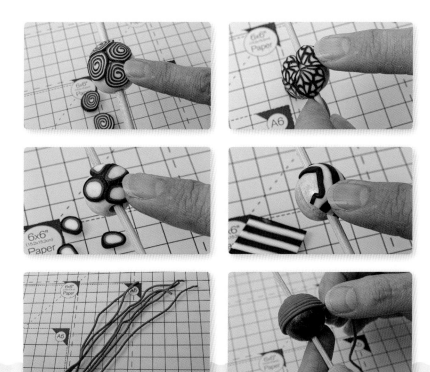

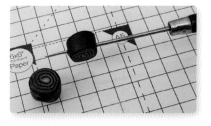

7. Cut two 1-cm pieces of the jelly cane and pierce them as indicated to make two beads.

8. Bake all the beads, following the clay manufacturer's instructions, allow them to cool and then apply a thin coat of varnish.

9. Allow the varnish to dry thoroughly. Attach a clasp at one end of the cord. Thread five small wooden beads with flower spacers between them onto the cord.

10. Thread the rest of the beads onto the cord in whatever order pleases you, but use a wooden bead with a flower spacer on either side between the clay beads. Make sure that the largest beads are in the centre.

11. End with five small, wooden beads and attach the other piece of the clasp to the cord.

Waste not, want not

I made this necklace using the clay that was left over after I had finished the string of rainbow beads. The bright, motley focal bead makes this piece really extraordinary.

MATERIALS AND TOOLS

Scraps of coloured clay (or create strips as explained on p. 62)

¼ block each of the following colours: neon orange, bright pink, purple, neon green, bright yellow

Metal pendant

Extra-thick embossing enamel (UTEE)

Heat gun

1 m fishing line (nylon thread)

32 bead caps

Crimp beads

Cord crimp ends

2 round rings

Fastener

METHOD

1. Make 16 small beads using the brightly coloured clay.

2. Combine all the scraps of clay and press it into the metal pendant.

3. Trim the edges neatly and sprinkle extra-thick embossing powder over the clay. Use a heat gun to heat it. Repeat the process until the bead has a glassy finish, and then bake all the beads according to the clay manufacturer's instructions.

4. Thread fishing line (nylon thread) through the metal pendant and fasten the two parts of the line using a crimp bead.

5. Thread the beads onto the line at fixed intervals by attaching a crimp bead to the line, followed by a bead cap, bead, bead cap and another crimp bead. Repeat until you have 8 beads on each side of the metal bead.

6. Trim away the excess fishing line (nylon thread) and attach a cord crimp bead at each end. Attach the rings and the fastener.

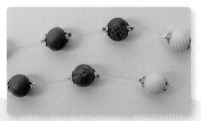

Millefiori and organza necklace

Organza, baked over this flat, clay bead, adds an interesting new dimension. Try this, using different colours to change the effect. Black and white would also look stunning and stylish.

MATERIALS AND TOOLS

Flower cane (see p. 48) or any other cane

¼ block each of the two matching colours

Matching, printed organza

Pasta machine and roller

Liquid polymer clay

Paintbrush

Silver ring

Cord and ribbon combination that matches the colours

Heat gun

Oval cookie cutter

Blades

Toothpick

METHOD

1. Condition the clay and roll each colour through the pasta machine on setting 1. Stack the two colours and run through the pasta machine again (setting 1).

2. Cut very thin slices from the millefiori cane and arrange them on the clay sheet.

3. Use a roller to flatten the floral slices, pressing them firmly into the clay.

4. Use a cookie cutter or a blade to cut out the pendant shape that you wish to make.

5. Pierce the top of the pendant.

6. Cut a piece of organza that is large enough to cover the entire pendant. Apply liquid polymer clay to the pendant and the organza. The liquid polymer clay prevents the organza from burning in the oven.

7. Bake the beads according to the clay manufacturer's instructions. When the organza-covered clay comes out of the oven, use the heat gun to make the liquid polymer clay translucent.

8. Trim the organza around the edges of the pendant and finish the edges. You can either use clay or simply sand and polish the edges. If you decide to use a clay finish, remember that the pendant will have to be baked again to cure the clay.

9. Fasten the ring in the hole at the top of the pendant, and thread the cord and ribbon through it.

10. The organza is not as prominent a feature on the black-and-white pendant as it is on the purple one. If you want it to feature more prominently, choose organza with a stronger, more distinctive design.

Quilt bracelet and earrings

The quilted effect achieved by using the cane on p. 32 reminded me of antique jewellery. I discovered these antique-looking findings in a bead shop. They complement the clay beautifully.

MATERIALS AND TOOLS

Quilt cane (see p. 32)

5 x bronze sliders

Liquid polymer clay

Piercing tool (awl)

Scrap clay for the edges of the earrings

4 x bronze decorative sliders

Thin elastic

16 x 6 mm bicone Swarovski crystals (burgundy)

4 x 4 mm bicone Swarovski crystals (olivine)

2 x bronze ear wires

36 small flower spacers

2 headpins

Jewellery glue

METHOD

1. Apply liquid polymer clay to the plain sliders.

2. Cut two slices from the quilt cane for each slider, press them together and into the slider.

3. Cut two thicker slices of the cane to use for the earrings. The back of the earrings consist of slices of the cane before they have been divided into four.

4. Pierce the squares that will be used for the earrings. If the square shapes distort when you pierce them, reshape them neatly.

5. Bake the beads according to the clay manufacturer's instructions and allow them to cool.

6. Shape a thin, green clay edge around the earring squares. Pierce them opposite the existing piercings, and bake them again.

7. Thread two strings of elastic through the holes of one clay-covered slider, and make a temporary knot in the elastic to prevent the beads from slipping off the string.

8. Thread a spacer, 6 mm crystal, and a spacer onto each string.

9. Thread the detailed spacer followed by a spacer, 6 mm crystal, and a spacer onto the string. Repeat this sequence until all the sliders have been used.

10. Make a double knot in both strings of elastic. Make sure that the knot is behind one of the sliders. Drip glue onto the knot to keep it from unravelling.

11. To make the earrings, thread a flower spacer, crystal, clay square, and a flower spacer onto the headpin.

12. Cut the pin shorter, make an eyelet and connect the ear wire to the eyelet.

Liquorice Allsorts necklace

The name of the necklace says it all. Because of the lovely, bright colours of the clay, this string of beads looks just like the real thing! Wear it with white and you will immediately catch the eye.

MATERIALS AND TOOLS

1 block black clay

¼ block each of the following colours: bright pink, bright yellow, white, brown, orange

Pasta machine or roller

Blades

Black tiger tail

Fastener and extension chain

4 crimp beads

2 shell ends

28 x 4 mm black glass crystals

2 x 12 mm twisted black glass crystals

METHOD

1. Use the bright yellow, pink, orange and black clay to make bull's eye canes: two canes with black centres wrapped in thick coloured layers; and three canes with thick, coloured centres wrapped in a layer of black.

2. To make the square sweetie beads, roll some of the colours through the pasta machine on setting 1, and cut 2 cm x 2 cm squares from the sheet. Shape the sweets by stacking squares of different colours and pressing the layers together.

3. Cut 1-cm slices from the canes and pierce the squares and slices to make the beads. Thread the beads onto toothpicks and arrange them carefully so that their shapes will not be distorted. Bake the beads according to the clay manufacturer's instructions.

4. Thread a crimp bead, shell end and another crimp bead onto black tiger tail.

5. Close the crimp bead firmly, and also close the shell end.

6. Attach the extension chain to the hook of the shell end and close the ring.

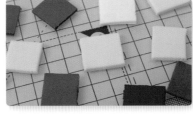

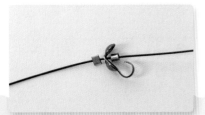

7. Thread a small, round, black bead, followed by the twisted black bead, another small black bead and a clay bead onto the tiger tail.

8. Now you can use any sequence, but each clay bead must be followed by a small, round, black bead.

9. Finish the string, reversing the order (mirror image) set out in step 4, and attach the fastener to the other end of the tiger tail.

Geometric necklace

Once again, the charming, bright colours of the clay inspired me to create this neckpiece.

MATERIALS AND TOOLS

Scraps of clay for the basic beads

¼ block each of the following colours: brown, orange, yellow, bronze, blue, red

Liquid polymer clay

Pasta machine and roller

30 cm bronze chain

7 bronze eye pins

4 bronze ball spacers

Small pliers

Bronze parrot fastener and ring

Extra-thick embossing enamel (UTEE)

Heat gun

Blades

Toothpicks

METHOD

1. Roll the scraps of clay through the pasta machine on setting 1. Cut two rectangles measuring 2 cm x 8 cm, and four rectangles measuring 2 cm x 6 cm.

2. Insert a toothpick 2 cm from the top of one of the large rectangles. Insert toothpicks 1,5 cm from the top edges of two of the smaller rectangles. Press the matching rectangles on top of the ones pierced by toothpicks.

3. Use a roller to roll across the areas where the toothpicks have been inserted, making sure that the toothpicks are pressed into the clay. This serves to make holes for the stringing of the beads.

4. Bake the rectangles according to the clay manufacturer's instructions, and condition all the coloured clay in the meantime. Roll the clay through the pasta machine on setting 3.

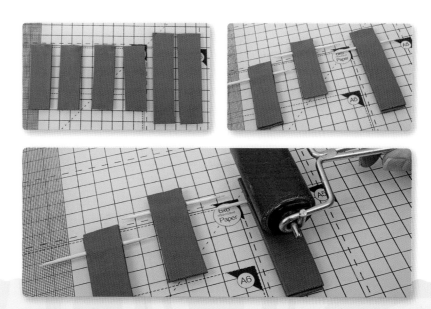

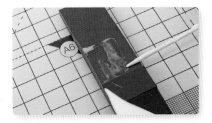

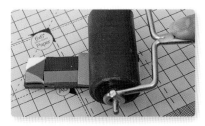
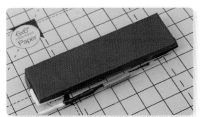

5. Apply liquid polymer clay to the baked rectangles. Cut geometrical shapes from the various colours of clay sheets and press these firmly onto the rectangles. Don't worry if some of the pieces of clay are too big – everything will be trimmed neatly.

6. Once the entire rectangle has been covered in coloured shapes, use a roller to roll over the clay to make sure that the colours meet and that there are no spaces.

7. Don't worry if the geometric lines are not well-defined and neat – remember, you are producing a unique, handmade piece. Place the rectangle face down, and trim the excess clay neatly along the edges.

8. Bake the rectangles according to the clay manufacturer's instructions and allow them to cool. Sand the sides until they are smooth.

9. Mix scraps of the brightly coloured clay, and roll it together.

10. Run the clay through the pasta machine on setting 3.

11. Apply liquid polymer clay to the edges of the rectangles and press the rolled out clay firmly onto the edges. Neatly trim the edges and pierce the side that has already been pierced.

12. Bake the rectangles according to the clay manufacturer's instructions and allow the clay to cool.

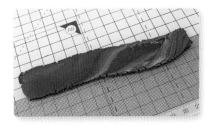

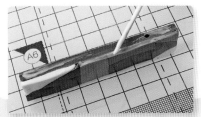
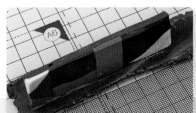
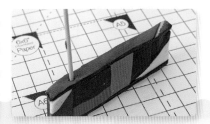

13. Apply liquid polymer clay to the rectangles, sprinkle thick embossing powder over them and use the heat gun to achieve a glassy finish.

14. Thread eye pins through all the ball spacers and make an eyelet at the end of each pin.

15. Thread the eye pins through the rectangles and make an eyelet at the end of each pin. Attach the rectangles and ball spacers in turn, positioning the longest rectangle in the centre.

16. Divide the chain into two and attach the ball spacers to each of the cut ends.

17. Attach a ring and parrot fastener to the end of the chain.

Millefiori flower necklace and bracelet

The millefiori canes described in the first part of the book can be used for a variety of projects. In this instance the cane works really well to make jewellery. The findings are a good match for the millefiori cane on p. 44.

MATERIALS AND TOOLS

Millefiori cane (see p. 44)

Pasta machine or roller

Blades

Silver metal pendant

Scraps of clay to fill the pendant

Scraps of clay matching the colours of the millefiori cane

2 x 6 mm brown miracle beads

6 x 4 mm brown miracle beads

4 x 3 mm orange miracle beads

50 cm silver chain

9 silver eye pins

4 antiqud sliders

5 x 4 mm light brown glass pearls

Silver clasp

METHOD

1. Roll the scraps of clay through the pasta machine on setting 1 and press it firmly into the metal pendant.

2. Mix scraps of the millefiori cane to achieve a marbled effect. Roll it through the pasta machine on setting 3. Cut a rectangle that is large enough to fit into the metal pendant. Also cut smaller rectangles that will fit into the sliders of the bracelet.

3. Cut a very thin slice from the millefiori cane and place it in the centre of the marble rectangle.

4. Reduce the milleriori cane, cut four very thin slices from the cane and arrange them on the marble rectangle as indicated.

5. Neatly trim the edges.

6. Cut slices from the reduced cane, arrange them on the small rectangles of the sliders, and flatten them using a roller.

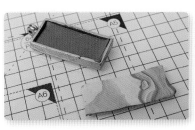

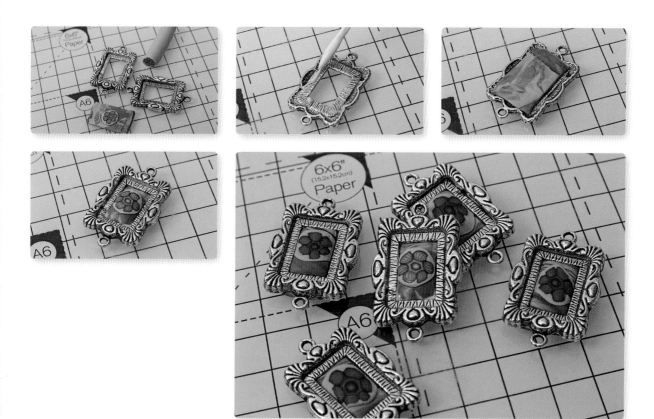

7. Apply liquid polymer clay to the backs of the silver sliders and press the rectangles containing the flowers, facing down, onto them.

8. Carefully apply pressure to the backs of the rectangles so that they protrude slightly at the front.

9. Bake the metal pendant and silver sliders according to the clay manufacturer's instructions.

10. Thread the glass pearls onto an eye pin and make an eyelet on the other end. Use the eye pins to attach the pearls and sliders.

11. Attach the two parts of the clasp to the bracelet, one on each end.

12. To make the necklace: thread 1 x 4 mm, 1 x 6 mm and 1 x 4 mm brown miracle beads onto an eye pin, and make an eyelet on the other end. Make two of these pins.

13. Pass a small piece of chain through the ring of the metal pendant and attach a brown beaded eye pin to either side of the chain.

14. Attach a 10-cm chain to the brown beads. Thread 1 x 3 mm orange, 1 x 4 mm brown, and 1 x 3 mm orange miracle bead onto an eye pin and make an eyelet on the other end. Attach this combination to the chain and attach a chain measuring 25 cm to the other side of the combination.

15. Make another eye pin using the orange-brown bead combination, and complete the necklace.

Necklace with silver pendant – two variations

This silver pendant immediately caught my eye in the bead shop. Not only could it make a subtle, soft pendant with polymer clay, but also a very bright one. It can also be very striking if you fill each hole of the pendant with a different colour.

MATERIALS AND TOOLS

Silver pendant

Pink, white, turquoise and brown clay – small pieces of each

White or blue ribbon and cord combination

Rings to attach the pendant to the cord

Liquid polymer clay

Pasta machine or roller

Blades

METHOD

1. Use the brown and blue clay to create a marbled effect and roll it through the pasta machine on setting 1. Roll the blue clay through the pasta machine as well.

2. Stack the two clay sheets and press them together firmly. Smooth the surface of the clay to force out all the air bubbles.

3. Apply liquid polymer clay to the back of the pendant and press the pendant firmly onto the clay.

4. Trim the excess clay using a blade.

5. Force the clay through one of the holes in order to attach the ring and bake the pendant according to the clay manufacturer's instructions.

6. Complete the necklace by attaching the ring and cord.

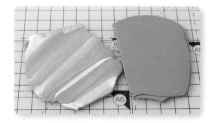

METHOD FOR PINK AND TURQUOISE PENDANT

1. Roll white clay through the pasta machine on setting 1. Apply liquid polymer clay to the back of the pendant and press the white onto it. Force the clay through one of the holes and bake the pendant following the clay manufacturer's instructions.

2. Press tiny bits of white, pink and turquoise clay into the holes on the front of the silver pendant. When you are satisfied with the result, bake the pendant according to the clay manufacturer's instructions and allow it to cool.

3. Complete the necklace by attaching the ring and cord.

Antique flower necklace

The classic simplicity of this necklace makes it really extraordinary. It is very delicate and feminine, and the earthy colours make it suitable to wear with just about any outfit.

MATERIALS AND TOOLS

Bronze pendant

¼ block each of bronze and gold clay

Rubber flower stamp

Brown acrylic paint

8 eye pins

40 cm bronze flower chain

Bronze clasp

2 round bronze rings

METHOD

1. Mix the bronze and gold clay to produce a more antique-looking colour. Flatten a small piece of the clay and press it onto the metal pendant. Use the rubber stamp to print a flower in the clay.

2. Bake the pendant according to the clay manufacturer's instructions. Allow it to cool and carefully apply brown paint to the flower design to define it. Wipe off excess paint.

3. Make four round and four oval beads using the mixed clay, pierce them and bake them according to the clay manufacturer's instructions. When the beads have cooled, thread each one onto an eye pin individually and make an eyelet at the other end.

4. Cut the flower chain exactly between two consecutive flowers. Reattach the two pieces of chain using an oval bead. Cut the chain between the next two consecutive flowers. Join the two pieces using a round bead.

5. Cut the chain between the following two consecutive flowers, attach a round ring to one side and attach the pendant to it. Complete the other half of the chain using the same steps.

6. Attach the clasp to the ends.

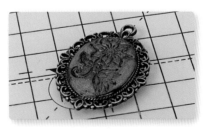

Suppliers

ITZ VAN ALLEZ

For clay

Website: **www.itzvanallez.co.za**

Address: 34 Jones St, Parow 7500

Tel: 021 911 0962

E-mail: surika@mweb.co.za

Online sales: www.crafts.bevan.co.za

VALUE BAKING SUPPLIES

For cookie cutters and texture plates:

Website: **www.valuesupplies.co.za**

Address: 25 Tarentaal Crescent, Okavango Industrial,
 Cape Town 8001

Tel: 021 981 0304

FILANI

For clay and all tools and equipment

Website: **www.polymerclay.co.za**

Address: Unit 15, Celie Office Park, Celie Road, Retreat,
 Cape Town 8001

Tel: +27 83 658 7500 (Paul) / +27 83 409 2301 (Phila)

Fax: 0866 103 844

E-mail: info@polymerclay.co.za

PNA

For clay

Most PNAs stock clay. To find your nearest branch, go to
 www.pna.co.za